A New National Security Strategy in an Age of Terrorists, Tyrants, and Weapons of Mass Destruction

Three Options Presented as Presidential Speeches

Lawrence J. Korb, Project Director

A Council Policy Initiative

Sponsored by the Council on Foreign Relations

The Council on Foreign Relations is dedicated to increasing America's understanding of the world and contributing ideas to U.S. foreign policy. The Council accomplishes this mainly by promoting constructive debates and discussions, clarifying world issues, and publishing *Foreign Affairs*, the leading journal on global issues. The Council is host to the widest possible range of views, but an advocate of none, though its research fellows and Independent Task Forces do take policy positions.

THE COUNCIL TAKES NO INSTITUTIONAL POSITION ON POLICY ISSUES AND HAS NO AFFILIATION WITH THE U.S. GOVERNMENT. ALL STATEMENTS OF FACT AND EXPRESSIONS OF OPINION CONTAINED IN ITS PUBLICATIONS ARE THE SOLE RESPONSIBILITY OF THE AUTHOR OR AUTHORS.

This volume is the sixth in a series of Council on Foreign Relations Policy Initiatives (CPIs) designed to encourage debate among interested Americans on crucial foreign policy topics by presenting the issues and policy choices in terms easily understood by experts and nonexperts alike. The substance of the volume benefited from the comments of several analysts and many reviewers, but responsibility for the final text remains with the project director.

Other Council Policy Initiatives:

Reshaping America's Defenses: Four Alternatives (2002), Lawrence J. Korb, Project Director; *Humanitarian Intervention* (2000), Alton Frye, Project Director; *Future Visions for U.S. Defense Policy* (1998; revised 2000), John Hillen and Lawrence J. Korb, Project Directors; *Toward an International Criminal Court* (1999), Alton Frye, Project Director; *Future Visions for U.S. Trade Policy* (1998), Bruce Stokes, Project Director.

Council on Foreign Relations Books, Task Force reports, and CPIs are distributed by Brookings Institution Press (1-800-275-1447). For further information about the Council or this paper, please write to the Council on Foreign Relations, 58 East 68th Street, New York, NY 10021, or call the Director of Communications at 212-434-9400. Visit our website at www.cfr.org.

CONTENTS

FOREWORD

From the fall of the Berlin Wall in 1989 to the fall of the Twin Towers in 2001, and even after the 2003 Iraq war, the United States has not had a consistent national security strategy that enjoyed the support of the American people and our allies. This situation is markedly different from the Cold War era, when the United States had a clear, coherent, widely supported strategy that focused on containing and deterring Soviet communist expansion.

The tragic events of September 11, the increase in terrorism, and possible threats from countries that are capable of developing weapons of mass destruction now make it imperative to develop a new security strategy to safeguard the United States. Americans are beginning to recognize the need for a vigorous debate about what that new strategy should be. Three approaches suggest themselves to us at the Council, each of which would lead our country in a different direction. In brief, these choices call for leveraging American dominance with preventive military action, creating stability by using American military superiority for deterrence and containment, and working toward a more cooperative, rule-based international system backed by American power that is used in genuine concert with U.S. friends and allies.

We are still far from agreement on which of these approaches to pursue. So, instead of establishing a CFR Task Force and seeking an unlikely consensus, we decided to employ another Council vehicle, which we call a Council Policy Initiative (CPI). It is designed to foster debate by making the best case for each of the alternatives. We've tried the same approach on defense policy twice before: the first time in 1998, to address concerns about the readiness of our forces to meet the challenges of the post–Cold War world, and again in 2002, in response to the new lineup of threats to homeland security after September 11. This third CPI builds on the defense strategies discussed in the previous two but also aims to define an overarching American national security policy to address the threats we face today.

The debate now stirring over the best path for U.S. national security policy to take is particularly important at this time in American history. Its outcome will have a profound impact not only on U.S. success in the war against terrorism, but also on transatlantic relations and the role of the UN in maintaining international peace and stability.

I would like to thank the primary author of this CPI, Larry Korb, senior fellow and director of the Council's National Security Studies Program, for directing the effort. Although this publication is called a Council Policy Initiative, it was really Larry's initiative, hard work, and perseverance that brought it to life.

Leslie H. Gelb
President
Council on Foreign Relations

ACKNOWLEDGMENTS

This Council Policy Initiative (CPI) could not have been completed without the efforts and contributions of several people. I would like to thank first and foremost Atman Trivedi, a Council intern and Columbia Law School student, who conducted research, worked on drafts, and corrected the manuscripts. Council President Les Gelb also played a major role in helping me crystallize the three options presented in this volume. Thanks also go to Patricia Dorff and Jennifer Anmuth, who did a terrific job of publishing the text, as well as to David Pacheco, Uday Ram, and Alex Tiersky, who graciously carried the CPI through the final stretch, and to Mike Peters, the director of the Council's Studies Program for his helpful comments. I also wish to extend my thanks to Lee Feinstein, deputy director of Studies, who helped to conceptualize this project and bring it to fruition. Thanks also go to Irina Faskianos, the Council's vice president for National and Outreach Programs, for taking this debate on the road to cities throughout the United States.

We are grateful for the generous support of three foundations, whose contributions and vision made this effort possible. The United Nations Foundation, which proposed this project to us in the winter of 2002, has provided generous financial support and on-the-ground talent in key cities around the country and in Washington, D.C. We wish to extend special thanks to UNF President Tim Wirth, who proposed this project to us, and to Phyllis Cuttino, UNF's vice president for public affairs. The Open Society Institute helped to leverage support for this effort from within the foundation community and also contributed generously to the project. We wish to thank, especially, Morton H. Halperin, OSI's Washington director, and Mimi Ghez, senior policy analyst, and to acknowledge the generous support of the Rockefeller Brothers Fund and Priscilla Lewis, program officer for the Peace and Security Program.

Finally, we also wish to thank the Carnegie Corporation of New York, and its program chair for International Peace and Security, David Speedie, for its support for the Council's national security programs of which this CPI is a part.

Lawrence J. Korb
Project Director

MEMORANDUM TO THE PRESIDENT

FROM: "The National Security Adviser"

SUBJECT: Implementation of the National Security Strategy: Alternative Policy Speeches

PURPOSE

From the fall of the Berlin Wall in 1989 to the fall of the Twin Towers in 2001, and even now after the Iraq war of 2003, the United States has not had a consistent national security strategy that enjoyed the support of the American people and our allies. This situation is markedly different from the Cold War era, when our nation had a clear, coherent, widely supported strategy that focused on containing and deterring Soviet communist expansion. The tragic events of September 11, the increase in terrorism, and threats from countries such as North Korea and, until recently, Iraq create an imperative once again to fashion and implement a coherent national security strategy that will safeguard our national interests.

It is always something of a challenge to reduce major policy directions into stark, concise options without distorting the arguments and without losing the flavor of real choices that inherently overlap to some degree. But there are genuinely different thrusts to the national security strategies being discussed within and outside the administration. We have discerned three approaches that we feel represent these different thrusts, each of which would lead our country in a different direction. In brief, these choices call for leveraging American dominance with preventive military action, creating stability by using American military superiority for deterrence and containment, and working toward a more cooperative, rule-based international system backed by American power that is used in genuine concert with our friends and allies.

The first of these policy thrusts is advocated mainly by those identified as "neoconservatives" and a number of conservatives as well; both groups are found principally within the Republican Party. Their argument holds that the most serious threats to American security come from the combination of terrorism, rogue states, and weapons of mass destruction (WMD). The temptation to try using these weapons against Americans is high for several reasons, including the fact that clearly identifying and punishing the attacker is inherently difficult. The United States is not going to be able to talk others out of developing these weapons and is also unlikely to be able to build an international coalition to help get rid of them. This country must therefore have both the capability and the will to use force preemptively, if necessary, against those states and groups that represent the most serious threats to U.S. security and the American way of life. Furthermore, the United States should be prepared to do this essentially on its own, unbound by the need for allies or United Nations (UN) approval. In the longer term, the United States must undercut any potential adversaries by ensuring the spread of free-market democracy throughout the world. Many contend that the first test of this policy was the war in Iraq.

The second thrust is associated with those generally called "moderates"—i.e., some moderately conservative Republicans and most moderate liberals within the Democratic Party. This approach holds that terrorism, rogue states, and weapons of mass destruction represent the most serious threats to U.S. security and the American way of life, but that these threats cannot be dealt with effectively in all places and every time through the unilateral use of American military force. The best way, if not the only way, to manage and eventually defeat these threats is by using American power in conjunction with international support. Although the United States alone can inflict military defeat on just about any state in the world, it will not have the capacity to turn military victory into a stable peace or to fully remove threats without ongoing international cooperation. To gain that international support will require the United States to take the views of others into account and to make serious efforts to contain and deter the threats before actually employing military force.

The third thrust is advocated primarily by people with a liberal approach, most of whom identify themselves as Democrats. Supporters of this policy point out that, although the short-term threats to U.S. security and the American way of life come from terrorists, rogue states, and weapons of mass destruction, the United States is also threatened by the longer-term effects of global poverty, growing lawlessness, and the increasing isolation of the country from like-minded states. Resort to force as the centerpiece of a national strategy, either by means of preventive war or through a dominant kind of deterrence, will not by itself be able to address either the near- or long-term threats. The United States must therefore change its emphasis from military force to diplomatic and economic cooperation. The United States needs to remain the strongest military power on earth, but it should also be an organizer of international coalitions aimed at solving major international problems and building world order.

You entered into this debate on September 17, 2002, when you formally outlined your new national security strategy. This National Security Strategy (NSS) was mandated by the 1986 Goldwater-Nichols Department of Defense Reorganization Act. According to that law, this document is supposed to be issued annually. Because of the change of administrations and the events of September 11, 2001, however, the strategy had not been updated since December 1999.

On December 12, 2002, you also made public the unclassified portions of National Security Presidential Directive 17 and Homeland Security Policy Directive 4 (NSPD-17/HSPD-4). This document was drafted by the National Security Council and approved by you in June 2002. It formed the basis for the NSS, and for your speeches at West Point and Fort Drum that same June. These two speeches laid the groundwork for the release of the NSS.

These documents, the NSS and NSPD-17/HSPD-4, which will be referred to throughout this memorandum as "the strategy," are the most detailed and comprehensive statements of how you intend to protect the national security interests of the United States in the post–September 11 world. In effect, they form the essence of what some have referred to as the "Bush Doctrine." Most elements of the media construe this doctrine to stand for the principle that this country will not hesitate to take anticipatory action to defend itself. They view it as a departure from the strategies of deterrence and containment carried over from the Cold War era by successive administrations. And they view the war on Iraq as the first manifestation of this policy.

Some analysts, like the diplomatic historian John Lewis Gaddis, have argued that the Bush Doctrine represents the most profound shift in U.S. grand strategy in the past 50 years and the first coherent statement of national security policy since the end of the Cold War. Others, including your secretary of state, have claimed that the items contained in the NSS and in NSPD-17/HSPD-4 are not radically different from existing policy.

Few mainstream policymakers, analysts, or commentators—either in the United States or around the world—have disagreed with the goals and strategic principles outlined in the strategy. There has been a great deal of controversy, both at home and abroad, however, about how these goals and principles would be implemented in specific cases, particularly when they seem to conflict with one another—for example, promoting democracy while conducting the war against terrorism, which requires cooperating with dictators. In addition, some people—even within the administration—support some aspects of the strategy while disagreeing with others. For example, some officials support the concept of preventive action but are wary of making the extension of democracy an explicit goal of U.S. national security policy. Still others support the promotion of democracy and individual rights but chafe at the perceived over-reliance on American military power to achieve these goals.

To clear up any confusion and allay concerns at home and abroad, we recommend that you give a major policy speech that lays out in specific terms how these concepts will be put into practice and how the different aspects of American foreign policy can be woven together in a broader intellectual framework. Such a framework will clearly set forth U.S. interests and values, embody your understanding of how today's world operates, clarify the U.S. role in it, and promulgate a set of strategies that can best serve those interests and values in light of the opportunities and constraints created by the new security environment. A great power such as the United States cannot afford to send mixed messages about its intentions, whether to its allies, to its competitors, or to its adversaries.

To help clarify your thinking on the ways that your strategy will be implemented and on how its parts relate to certain unifying themes and ideas, we present this memorandum. It is designed to make the best case for each of three plausible implementation strategies, providing relevant background information and discussing the strengths of each approach relative to the other two alternatives. Each strategy offers a distinct direction for American foreign policy and suggests a different set of priorities. This memo is followed by three draft speeches that elaborate on the strategic rationale for and flesh out the contents of each approach. The three specific policy options are as follows:

U.S. Dominance and Preventive Action. The most serious threats to American security come from the combination of terrorism, rogue states, and WMD. The temptation to try using these weapons against Americans is high for several reasons, including the fact that clearly identifying and punishing an attacker is inherently difficult. We are not going to be able to talk others out of developing these weapons, nor are we likely to be able to build an international coalition to help us get rid of these weapons. Therefore we must have both the capability and the will to use force against those states and the groups within them that represent the most serious threats to our security and way of life. And we should be prepared to do this essentially with U.S. military power alone, unbound by the need for allies or UN approval. In the longer term, we must undercut our potential adversaries by ensuring the spread of free-market democracy throughout the world.

Larger trends have conspired to make the threat posed by radicalism much greater in recent times. Given the rapid dissemination of destructive technologies, sensitive information, and capital flows in today's globalized world, threats from terrorist networks and rogue states can and will materialize more rapidly than in the past. Moreover, any attacks promise to be much more devastating if and when these actors get their hands on WMD. As the world's leading military and economic power, the United States is the most likely target of these terrorists and tyrants. In the face of, and in response to, these imminent dangers, it has not only the duty but also the legal and moral right to launch preemptive attacks, unilaterally if necessary. Common sense dictates that the government not stand idly by and wait to act until catastrophic attacks are visited upon the American people.

The United States has the unrivaled military and economic capability to repel these challenges to our security, but it must display the will to do so. To be able to carry out a strategy of preventive action, taking preemptive military action when necessary, this country must be a hegemonic power. The United States can protect its security and that of the world in the long run only by maintaining military dominance. Only America can effectively respond to the perils posed by terrorists, regional thugs, weapons proliferators, and drug traffickers. It can do the most to resolve problems created by "failed" states before they fester into major crises. And it alone can ensure that the world's sea lanes and skies are kept safe and open for free trade. But the array of challenges in its path requires military dominance and cannot be met on the cheap.

The ultimate goal of American foreign policy will be to use this power, alone if necessary, to extend free-market democracy around the globe. This is the only way in which the United States can deal with the long-term causes of terrorism. These terrorists come from countries that suffer from political repression, economic incompetence, and a broad lack of respect for the rule of law. And, contrary to what some believe, democracy and capitalism do not spread inexorably on their own. The United States therefore needs to assume a leadership role in spreading and accelerating the growth of free-market democracies that have been taking hold in the aftermath of the Cold War.

The vice president, the secretary and deputy secretary of defense, foreign policy hawks in both parties, and the neoconservative intellectual community all support these positions. They believe that this proactive strategy will enable the United States to use this moment of American primacy to make the world a safer and better place for the United States and its allies.

A More Stable World with U.S. Power for Deterrence and Containment. Terrorism, rogue states, and weapons of mass destruction do represent the most serious threats to U.S. security and the American way of life, but we cannot deal with these threats effectively in all places and every time through the unilateral use of U.S. military force. The best way, if not the only way, to manage and eventually defeat these threats is by using American power in conjunction with international support. Although the United States alone can inflict military defeat on just about any state in the world, we will not have the capacity to turn military victory into a stable peace or to fully remove threats without ongoing international cooperation. To gain that international support will require the United States to take the views of others into account and to make serious efforts to contain and deter the threats before actually employing military force.

History has demonstrated that even the most ruthless tyrants understand and respect the logic of robust containment and active deterrence. Indeed, one of your closest advisers argued in early 2000 that even if a rogue country ruled by a terrorist and tyrant like Saddam Hussein acquired WMD, its weapons would cause little tangible harm because any attempt to use them would bring national obliteration. When dictators have undertaken acts of aggression, it has been as a direct result of the United States' failure to communicate credibly its intent to retaliate. On those occasions, deterrence did not fail us; it was just poorly implemented.

A host of other problems would plague a strategy of U.S. dominance and preventive action. By making preemption a doctrine, the United States will encourage other states to legitimize their own aggression under the guise of defensive measures. Other states may already have begun to do just this, lowering the threshold for armed conflict and making the world less stable. Finally, by attempting to maintain military superiority and actively working to spread democracy and free markets throughout the world, this country will most likely overextend itself and take on the trappings of empire. Should the United States pursue an ambitious path of benign hegemony, it could lose track of its most important security priorities, suffer battle fatigue at home, and encourage a global backlash. We would then be likely to find ourselves in a situation very similar to the one that occurred in Vietnam some forty years ago, when successive American presidents committed national blood and treasure to a peripheral cause that was not essential to the overarching strategic goal of containing Soviet communist expansionism.

In the final analysis, the primary purpose of national security policy must be the narrower one of promoting stability, not the broader goal of extending free-market democracy. U.S. soldiers are not "social workers" equipped to conduct risky regime changes or undertake idyllic humanitarian interventions that are peripheral to our vital national interests. Rather than expend its energies on such futile strategies, this country should focus on the task of eradicating terrorist networks of global reach, while more vigilantly pursuing policies of robust containment and active deterrence that render outlaw regimes impotent.

Many members of the Senate Foreign Relations Committee and the House International Affairs Committee, officials at the State Department and the "old guard" of the foreign policy establishment, as well as most military leaders and many leading defense intellectuals support this position. For them, containment and deterrence can work against nation-states, no matter how repugnant their rulers. They are wary of the United States' losing its focus on the most critical threats to its security as it goes off on perceived utopian adventures abroad.

A Cooperative World Order. While the short-term threats to U.S. security and the American way of life come from terrorists, rogue states, and WMD, our country is also threatened by the longer-term effects of global poverty, growing lawlessness, and the increasing isolation of the United States from like-minded states. Resort to force as the centerpiece of a national strategy, either by means of preventive war or through a dominant kind of deterrence, will not by itself be able to address these short- or longer-term threats. The United States must therefore change its emphasis from military force to diplomatic and economic cooperation. We need to remain the strongest military power on earth, but we should also be an organizer of international coalitions aimed at solving major international problems and building world order.

This strategy recognizes the contribution that military power makes to U.S. security while acknowledging the limitations of relying too much on military power and maintains that this country's interests and values can best be pursued and sustained in the long term by working multilaterally with our allies and partners through international institutions. It does not mean to suggest that others have a veto over America's pursuit of its security, nor does it hold naïvely that the national interests of others can always be set aside to achieve consensus in favor of U.S. interests and values. But when it is possible, we should listen to our allies and partners, so that when the time comes for collective action, we will not have alienated our friends or even inadvertently created new enemies.

Such a policy will emphasize new synergies in global law enforcement, intelligence sharing, and efforts to thwart money-laundering to fight terrorists more effectively. It advocates the use of U.S. power to strengthen those norms and institutions designed to prevent the proliferation of WMD, including the nuclear Nonproliferation Treaty (NPT), the biological and chemical weapons conventions, and the Missile Technology Control Regime (MTCR). It also bolsters funding for programs that aim to reduce the spread of nuclear, biological, and chemical weapons materials and expertise in the former Soviet Union, such as the Nunn-Lugar Cooperative Threat Reduction Program. At the same time, this strategy strives to adapt existing cooperative security arrangements, such as the North Atlantic Treaty Organization (NATO), to deal with the new threat environment, while exploring new security-enhancing mechanisms with our friends in Asia. It integrates former adversaries, such as Russia and China, into an international system that supports U.S. values, and it emphasizes preventive diplomacy to quell conflicts before they erupt into major crises. Finally, this approach commits the United States to a leadership role in organizations that deal with economic, social, and health problems—problems that create a climate in which radicalism can flourish.

Although the use of force is certainly justified in self-defense, as is explicitly recognized in the UN Charter, it should be employed only when the threat is imminent and leaves no viable alternatives. In other words, striking first should be a tool of last resort, not a first option. Making unilateral preemption and military superiority the linchpins of U.S. national security policy will undermine international norms that favor nonaggression and weaken our own security in the long run by encouraging copycat behavior. Finally, many threats to the United States just cannot be resolved by unilateral force. It therefore makes little sense to try to maintain military superiority indefinitely, if doing so requires neglecting the nonmilitary components of our foreign policy and diverting funds from socioeconomic programs that keep this nation strong.

This position is supported by the internationalists in Congress and the State Department and by most members of the international legal and arms-control communities, as well as by a number of our key European allies and the other permanent members of the UN Security Council, not to mention the countries of the developing world. These groups contend that the United States can be more effective in enlarging the circle of free-market democracies through the use of diplomacy rather than through the use of brute military force. And for its supporters at home, this brand of multilateralism is not unalloyed altruism but the best way to serve the United States' enlightened self-interest.

Mr. President, we give you three speeches, each of which lays out one of the above options, so that you may decide how best to make the case to the public in favor of your own vision of American foreign policy. Each speech focuses exclusively on one overall direction for American foreign policy. Although the speeches are not written for experts, they are written by experts, so you and your speechwriters might want to polish the presentations. Obviously, in your actual speech, you may want to blend the choices to some degree, although you will find that some courses of action are incompatible with others, as each option proceeds from its own logic and assumptions about how the world operates. We sought a presentation that achieves conceptual purity in order to clarify and sharpen your choices and make more obvious the distinctions and trade-offs that exist among the three prevalent schools of thought.

These speeches specifically address how the United States will deal with particular threats to its national security and why it is necessary to act now. They do not discuss the particular military strategies and budgetary priorities needed to implement each option; as you know, those were the subject of an earlier memorandum. It is important to note, however, that each of the three alternatives will have a profound impact on this nation's defense spending. The current defense budget is about $400 billion and is projected to rise to about $500 billion over the next five years. If you embrace the option calling for U.S. dominance and preventive action, $500 billion a year will be inadequate to maintain the capability to launch essentially unilateral preventive military strikes against terrorists and tyrants who support them, or to maintain military dominance indefinitely. To implement this strategy, you would need to select the budgetary option we labeled enhanced defense in our earlier memo. This would add another $100 billion a year, or about 1 percent of our GDP, to the current defense budget, for a total of $600 billion a year. These additional funds would be used to increase the size of our active duty forces by 200,000 people, or 15 percent, to a total of 1.6 million, and close the $30 billion gap between current programs and projected budgets in our procurement account. This would permit us to replace our aging weapons in a timely fashion and accelerate the introduction of new technologies that give us greater precision and control on the battlefield. This $600 billion a year defense budget would not include the cost of actually waging preventive wars; as we saw in the war against Iraq, these costs could easily exceed $100 billion.

If you choose the deterrence and containment option, the current level of defense spending (already 10 percent above Cold War levels) should be adequate, provided that the secretary of defense is willing to follow up on his decision to eliminate the Crusader artillery system and cancel such other Cold War relics as the F/A-22 Raptor, the RAH-66 Comanche helicopter, and the Virginia class nuclear-powered attack submarine. Elimination of these programs would provide savings that could be used to transform the military, that is, create technologically sophisticated combat units that would be lighter, quicker, and more lethal than the current force.

If you choose to pursue a cooperative world order approach, you would be able to hold defense spending at its current level of $400 billion over the next five years and still safeguard the nation's security because we would not be attempting to meet the array of existing threats by ourselves. Instead, we would be taking the initiative to build international institutions and alliances in a new cooperative effort that rallies our friends and allies to deal with these common problems and use the funds that are projected to go to the defense budget to increase bilateral and multilateral foreign aid. In our earlier defense memo, we labeled this option the "cooperative security approach."

BACKGROUND

At the dawn of the Cold War, the executive branch initiated the practice of publicly articulating its national security strategy. The most well known of these early articulations was George Kennan's 1947 "X" article in *Foreign Affairs*, which provided the rationale for the containment strategy that became the cornerstone of U.S. foreign policy throughout the Cold War. This strategy was codified the following year by the Truman administration's National Security Council Document 68 (NSC-68).

The practice of issuing national security strategies did not become routine, however, until the Nixon administration released an annual State of the World Report. (During the Kennedy and Johnson administrations, the best rationale for U.S. national security policy was actually contained in the secretary of defense's "Annual Report to the Congress.") Congress made the submission of a national security strategy mandatory as a matter of law when, as part of the 1986 Goldwater-Nichols Department of Defense Reorganization Act, it required the president to report regularly on this subject to Congress and the American people. This law stipulates that the report be made annually, and that a new administration must release its strategy publicly within its first five months in office, a deadline that was not met by either of the last two administrations faced with this requirement.

Moreover, the outgoing Clinton administration did not issue a strategy document in its last year in office, and your NSS was not released until September 17, 2002, some 20 months after you came into office. Thus your NSS was the first public release of a strategy document in nearly three years. Its importance was magnified by the fact that it was your administration's first strategic policy pronouncement in the aftermath of September 11. And even if we had met the congressionally mandated deadline and released your NSS in June 2001, the events of September 11 would have made that report obsolete to some degree.

You subsequently articulated the key concepts of the NSS in your State of the Union address in January 2002 and in your speeches at West Point and Fort Drum in June 2002. Some of the ideas in the NSS are also reflected in the Defense Department's Quadrennial Defense Review (QDR), which was released three weeks after September 11, 2001.

A useful way to begin the analysis of your strategy documents is to compare the ideas contained in them to the last NSS, to your own campaign statements, and to the policies that you pursued in office prior to September 11, 2001. In President Clinton's final NSS, released in December 1999, his administration outlined three goals for the country. They said the purpose of the U.S. national security strategy was to promote security, to bolster America's economic prosperity, and to promote democracy and human rights around the world.

President Clinton recognized that military force might be necessary in situations that pose a threat to our national interests, but his NSS laid down a number of conditions that circumscribed its use. The former president argued that military forces should be brought in only if their use advances U.S. interests, if they are likely to accomplish the stated objective, if the costs and risks of their deployment are commensurate with the interests at stake, and if other nonmilitary means are incapable of achieving our goals. And the Clinton NSS emphasized that the United States would act in concert with the international community whenever possible.

The previous administration was not opposed to military interventions on humanitarian grounds, as witnessed by the U.S. uses of force in Haiti, Bosnia, and Kosovo. Perhaps haunted by the low-tech slaughter that unfolded in Rwanda, President Clinton's views gradually evolved to the point where he believed that the world community ought to stop genocide and ethnic cleansing—and the United States should assume the leadership role in doing so, if necessary. This perceived newfound willingness to intervene on moral and humanitarian grounds led some commentators to discern a "Clinton Doctrine."

In your successful 2000 campaign, you opposed such ad hoc interventions and "nation-building," instead calling for a more humble American approach to world affairs. You branded China and Russia "strategic competitors" rather than "strategic partners," as you intended to focus your foreign policy efforts on preventing the emergence of a rival great power. Once in office you opted out of several multilateral arrangements, including the Kyoto Protocol on global warming, the Biological Weapons Convention (BWC), and the International Criminal Court (ICC); talked about withdrawing American military forces from the Balkans and the Sinai Peninsula; and refused to follow through on the diplomatic initiatives in North Korea and in the Middle East that you had inherited from the Clinton administration. As one of your closest advisers wrote, your administration was intent on "proceed[ing] from the firm ground of the national interest and not from the interest of an illusory international community." You also adopted a much more confrontational approach toward China, particularly after that nation forced an American P-3 reconnaissance plane to land on Hainan Island, held the crew captive for several days, and refused to allow the crew to fly the plane home.

Not surprisingly, given the events of September 11, your NSS and NSPD-17/HSPD-4 strike quite a different tone from the previous administration's statements, your own campaign pronouncements, and the policies your administration pursued prior to September 11. The new documents state that the objectives of our strategy are to defend, preserve, and extend the peace, and that the United States will accomplish these three goals by fighting terrorists and tyrants, building good relations among the great powers, and encouraging free and open societies on every continent.

From the end of the Cold War through September 11, 2001, American foreign policymakers assumed that there would be no major disruptions in the international system, that there was no need to go out of the way to achieve great-power cooperation, and that, while the country should promote democracy and free markets, doing so was neither a strategic nor a moral imperative, nor did it need to do so on every continent. We did not want to create the perception that the United States was intent on global messianism or turn the traditional business of foreign policy into a more ambitious agenda that some decry as "social work."

Although some concern has been expressed about the goals of the NSS, they continue to resonate with most of the American people and with our allies, especially in light of the events of September 11. For the most part, both appreciate your willingness to state bluntly and openly what has long been the philosophical underpinning of American foreign policy. With the exception of the "deterrence and containment" camp, most Americans seem to agree that peoples everywhere desire the blessings of political and economic freedom, and, while we should take care to account for some diversity of approaches, democracy and free markets are generally laudable goals worth promoting.

In contrast, there has been quite a bit of controversy about the specific steps the United States will take to achieve these goals and whether the different components of the strategy come into conflict with one another. In addition, because you insisted that the document be short (mercifully, it ran only 31 pages), it does not deal in depth with some issues that are of legitimate national security concern to Congress, the American people, our allies, and our potential competitors.

As many analysts (from organizations as diverse as the Brookings Institution and the Heritage Foundation) have correctly noted, the strategy does contain four major innovations that make it markedly different from previous strategic documents. First, your NSS raises global terrorist networks and outlaw regimes to first-order, existential threats to the security of the United States and to the stability of the international political system. Prior to September 11, there seemed to be a general consensus within this administration that our key priority was to manage relations with the other great powers in order to prevent the emergence of new rivalries with old foes, particularly China. While a significant concern, recalcitrant regimes and terrorists were not perceived as threats of the same magnitude. They were viewed more as pawns in a geostrategic game of chess run by the great powers. But in today's changed climate, the NSS argues, the reactive strategies of deterrence and containment, which enabled this country to safeguard its security from the end of World War II through September 10, 2001, are no longer sufficient. Most of your national security team argued that those strategies will not alone succeed against either the shadowy terrorist networks that operate without any readily identifiable addresses or the radical regimes that secretly sponsor them. Accordingly, preemption must assume a greater role in this dangerous and uncertain era.

Second, the new strategy makes it clear that our military forces must remain dominant for the foreseeable future. Previously, in the 1990s, the United States structured its armed forces in accordance with a military strategy that required an ability to confront two major regional contingencies (MRCs) simultaneously. The Quadrennial Defense Review (QDR) of September 30, 2001, by contrast, emphasized deterrence in four major theaters, backed by the ability to swiftly defeat two aggressors in the same time frame while preserving the option of marching on the capital of one of the major aggressors and replacing its regime, if absolutely necessary. Neither the Department of Defense nor Congress explicitly embraced the idea that our forces had to be strong enough to dissuade our political adversaries from pursuing a military buildup aimed at surpassing or rivaling the power of the United States. They were content to rely on the old standbys of deterrence and containment. In fact, as you noted in your campaign and discovered on taking office, there was some doubt as to whether the Pentagon could even execute the two-MRC strategy.

Moreover, a policy of military dominance was disavowed by the previous Bush administration in 1992, when it became publicly known that some members of the Pentagon's civilian leadership were about to recommend such a policy. At that time, many observers, including the first President Bush and his national security adviser, viewed the strategy as somewhat arrogant, so it was quickly jettisoned. As you know, a number of individuals who now hold high positions on your national security team, including your vice president and secretary of defense, produced a 90-page blueprint in the fall of 2000 for transforming America's military and the nation's global role. This report, released by the Project for the New American Century, argued that the United States should not only attain and maintain military dominance, but it should also project it with a worldwide network of forward operating bases over and above our already extensive overseas deployments. These advisers believe that maintaining the dominance of our armed forces is necessary to preventing the emergence of any rival power and have concluded that others will not dare embark on futile arms races once they realize the preponderance of our military power.

Third, the new strategy emphasizes cooperation among the great powers in order to preserve a unified front in the war on terrorism. It advocates that this cooperation be carried out under the aegis of American leadership. Unlike previous presidents' statements, particularly those enunciated during the Cold War, the new strategy assumes that other great powers—China, Russia, India, Japan, and the European Union—prefer the international system to be managed by a single hegemon like the United States because its impulses are relatively benign and because it stands for certain values that are shared by most states.

Your strategy conveys an understanding that there are some things, like armed forces to maintain the peace and funds for financial bailouts, that only this country can provide because of its unrivaled military and economic capabilities. And it reflects a conviction that the United States does not seek to acquire foreign territories, subjugate other peoples, or alter the international status quo in any way that is hostile to the legitimate aspirations of freedom-loving citizens of the world—and that our most important allies and strategic partners will recognize this to be the case. In short, the strategy postulates that the United States does not wish to create an empire and maintains that others will take our words at face value. More important, it makes the critical assumption that the great powers are united in their perception of a common threat—the terrorists and the tyrants who support them—for the first time since the end of the Cold War. It maintains that we can set aside our lingering differences with other great powers to forge a common front as part of the war on terrorism.

Fourth, a security strategy enunciates, for the very first time, a policy that specifically calls for removing the root causes of terrorism and tyranny. This strategy document commits the United States to seeking to extend free-market democracy everywhere, even to pockets of the world such as the Middle East, where many nations—sometimes with our own grudging support or acquiescence—have resisted its spread. In recent months, this strategy has taken concrete shape in the form of our calling for regime change in the Palestinian Authority and pursuing it in Iraq, as well as pressing traditional allies such as Egypt and Saudi Arabia to enact democratic reforms. The military operations for disarming Iraq will come into conflict, at least in the short term, with the other goals we have for the region, as we work to build a local consensus in favor of our Iraq policy. But, in the long term, disarming and democratizing Iraq could actually further the democratization of the rest of the Middle East, if we can successfully establish that country as a blueprint for other states in the region to follow.

But, as many of these same analysts have noted, the controversy over the means of implementing the goals and innovations in your NSS also arises in four specific areas. The first area, which is the one that has received the most attention, is the emphasis on pre-emption (as opposed to deterrence and containment) as the key component of your NSS. In the strategy document and in your West Point speech, you emphasized that we cannot let our enemies strike first. But some observers, such as Clinton's deputy national security adviser, James Steinberg, have accused your administration of failing to clarify in the strategy document exactly which enemies it has in mind. In their view, it is unclear whether a policy of preemption applies only to terrorists or also to the rogue states that harbor them. If it also applies to rogue regimes, they ask if the policy includes all outlaw states, only the "axis of evil" states, or just a particular member of the latter category. Some are also confused about the criteria that will be used to decide whom and when to preempt. Finally, more recent press reports have speculated that preemption might even include a first strike with nuclear weapons against "hard targets."

One of your closest advisers sought to clear up some of this confusion in a speech to the Manhattan Institute in New York City on October 1, 2002. Among other things, she tried to make clear that we are not proposing to abandon the traditional concept of deterrence. Our strategy, in fact, explicitly endorses deterrence, stating flatly that the military must be able to deter threats against U.S. interests, allies, and friends. She also sought to assure your administration's critics that the preemptive use of force would be applied in a careful and considered manner. Preemption, she said, would come only after all other means, including diplomacy, had been exhausted, and in response to a grave threat, for which the dangers of waiting outweighed the risks of taking action.

Some commentators have asked, however, if all this talk of preemption might undermine strategic stability in a crisis by providing foes with incentives to lash out at the United States first, rather than wait for a debilitating first strike by us. They think that preemption might undermine deterrence by encouraging countries to adopt precarious "launch-on-warning" force postures and undertake a "race to the button" in a crisis, thereby potentially unleashing their weapons systems in advance of a destructive preemptive U.S. strike against them.

Moreover, if the United States preserves the right to preempt when it believes that its enemies are poised to strike against it, our critics ask what is to prevent India from employing the same doctrine to justify a preemptive strike against Pakistan, or China against Taiwan, or Russia against Georgia. Some observers point out that high-level Indian and Russian leaders have already made statements approving of the value of "anticipatory self-defense" after the release of your NSS. The analysts' concern, which we ourselves identified in the NSS, is that other countries could publicly adopt similar defensive strategies as pretexts for aggression.

More broadly, the preemption doctrine elicits concern in foreign capitals and in the halls of international organizations that the foreign policy of this nation has undergone a radical revision in the aftermath of September 11. Our allies and partners fear that this doctrinal innovation signals the birth of a new era in which an enraged America is intent on revising the international status quo to its own liking. They have expressed the fear that the United States has given itself a green light to use its vast forces hastily against recalcitrant nations, so as to remake them in America's own image. In short, critics see this strategy as ushering in a new age of American imperialism.

The second area that requires our concentrated attention is reconciling the tension between promoting the ideals of democracy and free enterprise, on the one hand, and waging the war against terrorism, on the other. Many of the states that have been critical to cracking down on al-Qaeda are among the most flagrant violators of the universal principles espoused in the strategy. Nations such as Uzbekistan, Tajikistan, Turkmenistan, and Pakistan, which were so crucial to our initial success in Afghanistan against al-Qaeda and the Taliban, rarely hold free elections and regularly trample on the individual rights of their citizens. Moreover, in the recent war against Iraq, none of the regional countries that allowed us to base coalition forces on its soil was a democracy. Indeed, democratic Turkey would not let us use its territory to attack Iraq.

In the Middle East, two of our critical allies in the war on terrorism, Saudi Arabia and Egypt, do not share our respect for human rights and the rule of law. In fact, some allege that the authoritarian posture of the Saudi regime and its ineffectual economic policies have created a breeding ground for young radicals, among them fifteen of the terrorists who carried out the September 11 attacks. The Saudis' permissive attitude toward radicalism—and, in particular, their lax policing of charitable organizations that laundered money for the September 11 attacks—has come under heavy fire. While cozying up to Washington in its official diplomacy, Egypt too continues to editorialize in shrill tones against American interests in its state-run press and to pursue repressive policies toward its peoples.

Finally, two other great powers—China and Russia—continue to crack down rather viciously on their respective separatist rebel movements, both of which have their own legitimate complaints against their governments. Each nation has justified violating the human rights of its purported citizens by calling these insurgents terrorists.

Waging a successful campaign against terrorists and their state sponsors requires the support of a number of illiberal actors, but in securing this support we pay a price in terms of convincing the American public, our allies, and others around the world that we are fully committed to the goals of promoting democracy and economic freedom.

The third issue that demands more clarity is the role of existing alliances vis-à-vis what you call "coalitions of the willing," or ad hoc coalitions. Your NSS remarks that the United States is committed to supporting long-standing institutions such as the UN, the World Trade Organization (WTO), the Organization of American States (OAS), and NATO. But the NSS also calls for creating coalitions of the willing, as we did in the war against Iraq, to deal with specific threats. The former language suggests a willingness to consult with our traditional allies and partners, while the latter implies that this country alone determines the mission in any given circumstance, and others can hop aboard if they wish—but whether they do so or not is largely irrelevant to us. If America systematically chooses to bypass established organizations such as the UN in favor of ad hoc coalitions, then it risks their increasing obsolescence in the face of today's new challenges. By the same token, these traditional institutions may constrain American power and frustrate the pursuit of our national interests amid interminable consultations with those whose express purpose it is to render less significant the U.S. advantages in military and economic power—as we recently witnessed in the debate within the UN Security Council over a second resolution authorizing the use of force to disarm the Iraqi regime.

The strategy offers little guidance as to which is the preferred arrangement and when each approach should be used. It also begs the question of what damage will be done to existing multilateral organizations, such as NATO, if they are routinely bypassed, as NATO was in the war against the Taliban and al-Qaeda in Afghanistan and the UN was in the war against Iraq. Our European allies played a minimal part in the military campaign in Afghanistan, despite their first-ever invocation of Article V of the North Atlantic Treaty, which stipulates that an attack on one member is an attack on all.

There are also questions as to whether the different parts of the strategy may contain internal tensions or contradict one another. Many individuals, even those holding high posts within your administration, embrace one or two components of the NSS but not all three. For example, a number of supporters of a preventive-war strategy do not endorse the idea of enlarging the number of free-market democracies. For them, our strategy should focus on the narrower, more conservative goal of promoting international stability. They equate the extension of free-market democracy with the program of nation-building, which they say requires American soldiers to play the unaccustomed role of global sheriff. You were opposed to this more ambitious agenda in the election campaign, expressing concerns about overextending our resources, diminishing our troops' morale and readiness for major crises, and unnecessarily creating resentment among those countries that fear this nation will use its immense power to recast the world in Uncle Sam's image.

Some within your administration not only do not wish to see American power deployed to support purely humanitarian operations like those in Haiti or Somalia, but they also oppose policies of regime change toward rogue states for the same reasons. They prefer to wait and keep our powder dry and our footprints barely visible until one of those outlaw regimes commits an act of aggression. This cautious approach, supported by a number of military leaders at the Pentagon, is said to keep our forces strong enough to respond to the real challenges to our vital national interests and increase the likelihood that war will be waged with significant popular approval.

Others who support preemption and the extension of democracy are worried that the concept of military dominance may prove a recipe for fiscal disaster, in effect giving the Pentagon the key to the back door of the Treasury. They believe that the military should receive only what is necessary to implement the goals outlined in the Pentagon's QDR. Proponents of this view can cite the fact that military spending has now outstripped other spending on foreign affairs by a ratio of more than sixteen to one. Our defense spending has already accelerated rather dramatically under your administration, from slightly less than $311 billion in fiscal year 2001 to more than $400 billion at present. This means that the United States already accounts for 40 percent of the world's military expenditures.

THE OPTIONS

Here are some crucial guideposts to keep in mind as you read the distilled discussion of the options below and the draft speeches that follow:

- The speech you would actually give to Congress, the UN, or another interested and involved group, such as the Council on Foreign Relations or the American Enterprise Institute, would likely be more general than the drafts provided here. It would probably also blend various elements from the other speeches. The secretaries of state, defense, and homeland security, as well as the director of central intelligence, would be responsible for further educating the public as to the rationale behind your choices.

- All the options discuss the role of international institutions, norms, and laws in foreign policy. Their significance is most comprehensively discussed in option three, however, which we brand the "cooperative world order" perspective. Similarly, all of the options deal with the role of preemption in foreign policy, but its merits are most thoroughly considered in the option of "U.S. dominance and preventive action." Finally, while all of the options also deal with the role of deterrence and containment, this policy is relied on and discussed most completely in the second option, "deterrence and containment," although to a significant degree the "cooperative world order" approach falls back on these traditional strategies as well.

OPTION ONE: U.S. DOMINANCE AND PREVENTIVE ACTION

The fall of the Berlin Wall and the collapse of the World Trade Center and the western wall of the Pentagon may be viewed as the bookends of a transition period that spanned from the end of the Cold War through the beginning of our general struggle against new forms of radicalism. During that transition period, there were serious disagreements about the nature of the international system in the post–Cold War world.

Some argued that the end of the Cold War meant the "end of history"—that is, the triumph of liberal, democratic values that would be embraced globally with little serious effort by the United States. Others trumpeted the "obsolescence of war" and the dawning of a "new world order" when the Soviet empire peacefully expired, while still others were less optimistic, foreseeing a "clash of civilizations" as different cultures and societies butted heads. Then a series of ethnic conflicts in "failed" states in the early and mid-1990s convinced some that this lethal combination of ethnic hatred with poor or nominal governance presaged a "coming anarchy." Then, toward the end of the 1990s, still others concluded that the forces of globalization had permanently replaced the endless cycles of security competition among nation-states. They argued that at a time when barriers to trade and capital flows were falling, global markets knitted together by information technology were now more relevant than nation-states and traditional military power.

September 11 changed all that. We now know that this great nation of ours is vulnerable. For the first time in our history, an enemy has overcome our formidable geographic advantage to visit large-scale destruction on the U.S. mainland. The threats we face today come less from powerful states than from weak or small ones; less from large, sophisticated militaries than from shadowy bands of terrorists capable of wreaking havoc on this nation, our allies, and the world financial system. There is no longer any doubt that, at the current time and for the foreseeable future, we face an existential threat to our security. This threat is as great as any we have ever encountered throughout our history, even during World War II and the Cold War. In essence, we are in the midst of a fourth world war.

This new, threatening environment requires an equally novel, bold, strategic vision that captures today's realities and capitalizes on our unique capabilities to protect this great nation. We must proactively use our current position of unparalleled strength and influence—what some have labeled the "unipolar moment"—to create an international system that protects our interests and values. American primacy may not last forever, so the time is now to use our power to create a safer, better world. We can do this most effectively if we adopt a strategy of dominance and preventive action that makes the unilateral use of force, including preemption, the bedrock of the U.S. national security strategy.

No other nation or international body combines hard military and economic power with the will to deal with the grave threats posed by terrorists and tyrants. Their next attack on our nation, our interests, or our allies is very likely to involve nuclear, biological, or chemical weapons. If we wait for these threats to materialize fully, we will have waited too long. We owe it to the American people not to resort to the wishful thinking that these terrorists and tyrants will be deterred by traditional means. They were not deterred on September 11 and are not likely to be deterred in the future.

Nor can we expect international organizations or our allies to adequately protect our interests and values. Historically, when this country has hesitated in rising up to meet incipient security challenges, it has found that the dangers do not go away but grow. Throughout the last century, this proved to be the case, beginning with World Wars I and II and stretching through the ethnic conflicts of the 1990s. And when others have failed to suppress violence and instability, it has been the United States that has had to enter the fray to restore peace and stability. Now, as radicalism begins to intersect with destructive technologies, we can no longer afford to let the dangers gather on our doorstep.

Finally, given the nature of the threat we face, this strategy is not only legal under any common-sense definition of international law, it is moral as well, even according to the standards of "just war" theory. Nor is it entirely a new strategy; over the course of our history, many presidents have resorted to preemption to safeguard our national security.

To be able to sustain a strategy of preventive war, we must remain the world's only superpower. We must therefore maintain our military dominance, regardless of the cost. At present, our conventional and nuclear military strengths are beyond challenge, and we must keep them that way. To put it bluntly, our national security must be rooted in the preeminence of our military power and in our willingness to use that power to protect U.S. security.

This country should not allow itself to be tied down by international agreements or institutions. At a time when the danger is great, we cannot accept the fate of Gulliver in the land of the Lilliputians. Our hegemony is acceptable to most of the international community, even the great powers, because it is linked to universal values. As you noted in your State of the Union address in January 2003, these values are a gift from God to humanity, not from the American people to the rest of the world.

Once we establish the peace, we must go further to secure and extend it for future generations of Americans. If we content ourselves with defeating the terrorists and tyrants, but do little to replace their radical visions of society with something better, we will have squandered our unipolar moment. In short, we will never remove the root causes of terrorism and tyranny unless we work actively to spread free-market democracy throughout the world. To paraphrase President Woodrow Wilson, we must make the world safe for democracy if we intend to prevent another September 11.

Peace-loving peoples everywhere cherish the benefits of political and economic freedom. Through the battles against Hitlerism, fascism, militarism, and communism of the last century, our way of life proved to be the most successful. Even if this great country occasionally fails to live up to its ideals, our system of democracy and economic choice is the best one to serve the demands of human dignity. The freedoms you have spoken of are universal ones, shared and revered by peoples worldwide. And only this system of governance can extend the peace that Americans of all generations have worked so hard to create.

All three of these components—the use of military force, alone and preemptively if need be; military dominance; and democracy promotion—work seamlessly together. As in the case of building a three-legged stool, one cannot construct a sustainable policy based on only one or two of these components and expect the preventive-action strategy to hold together. Maintaining this country's military dominance is a necessary condition for a strategy that emphasizes the use of force in defense of our national security. And the first two legs of this option will collapse under their own weight without a complementary strategy that seeks to enlarge the circle of free-market democracies.

Advantages

- Adopts a proactive, coherent, and interconnected strategy that most vigorously responds to the existential threats to the United States posed by terrorist networks with a global reach and the "axis of evil" states.

- Pursues a strategy that takes best advantage of America's unrivaled military and economic power to act decisively at a time when this country is most vulnerable.

- Allows the United States to play a dominant role in the international system; ensures that our interests and values are not subordinated to those of other organizations or alliances that might have a different agenda than ours because they seek to constrain our power and influence or because they are not as likely to be the targets of terrorists and tyrants.

- Enables the United States to act unilaterally but for global ends. If, acting alone, this country destroys global terrorist networks such as al-Qaeda or removes a tyrant such as Saddam Hussein who threatens an entire region, it is, in essence, promoting global interests. And while some nations might publicly complain about unilateral preemption, in reality they will be glad that these threats have been effectively dealt with by someone else, without their having to sacrifice too much of their own blood and treasure.

Disadvantages

- Runs the risk of "imperial overstretch"—that is, exhausting our scarce resources by taking on too many simultaneous international commitments, which may create battle fatigue among the American people, Congress, and our allies.

- Could require massive increases in defense spending at a time when the federal budget is already running huge deficits and there are large competing claims, both at home and abroad, on discretionary funds.

- Regime change as part of a policy of extending democracy could undermine our ability to wage a successful war against terrorism because we need the assistance of many authoritarian regimes in the short run.

- Allows other nations to justify aggressive wars under the pretext of preventive war.

- Risks creating a backlash among our strategic competitors and even our European allies, who view our pursuit of military dominance as the beginning of an American empire and who could seek to balance American power either separately or together.

- Creates uncertainty about our intentions among our allies and adversaries, at home and abroad, if the United States fails to back up the sweeping rhetoric in the strategy and presidential statements with decisive action in every case.

Political Impact

- The hawks in Congress and the neoconservative members of the foreign policy establishment will welcome the strategic clarity and sound logic of this approach. They will see this as a natural byproduct of the unipolar world that is likely to exist for the foreseeable future but that will eventually come to an end. Opposition will come from realists worried about the United States' becoming the global sheriff. Multilateralists will be concerned about this country's bypassing international institutions and creating new international legal precedents that in their view will invite aggression by others.

- Military leaders in the Navy, the Air Force, and the Marine Corps will support the idea of preventive war, but the Army brass will be apprehensive about occupying countries after the attacks and will have some concerns that American troops may have to serve prolonged peacekeeping functions. All the military services will support the idea of dominance, as it will justify very large defense budgets for the indefinite future.

- The State Department and our allies will be concerned about this option because it will mark such a dramatic shift in the way that the United States conducts itself in the world. They fear that preemption will create a new standard for judging international behavior and that the attempt to maintain American hegemony will stir up a backlash even among our allies. More broadly, they will have concerns that we are relying too much on the military, to the exclusion of diplomatic tools in the foreign policy tool kit.

- Among the general public, support cannot be expected without vigorous presidential leadership that clearly enunciates why the United States must act preemptively and unilaterally and why this country at this stage in its history must implement Wilson's dream of making the world safe for democracy. Realists and liberal segments of the American populace will be concerned that this approach signals a new and unprecedented willingness to build an American empire.

OPTION TWO:
A MORE STABLE WORLD WITH U.S. POWER FOR DETERRENCE
AND CONTAINMENT

While the United States certainly has the legal and moral right to wage a preventive war against terrorists who are planning to attack this nation, its allies, or its interests, anticipatory self-defense should not be elevated to the status of a doctrine. Preemptive military action against terrorists is only one component of the war on terrorism. The best way to preempt attacks by terrorists is to work with other nations to share intelligence about these groups, dry up their financial assets, and arrest them before they are in a position to cause harm. In fact, in working with law enforcement and intelligence officials around the globe since September 11, we have already preempted dozens of attacks by arresting more than three thousand suspected terrorists.

The neoconservatives who support the first option are right to a limited extent—that preemption is not a new policy for this country. The Clinton administration established an Office of Counterproliferation in the Pentagon and actually contemplated a preemptive attack against North Korea's nuclear reactors in 1994. President Reagan's invasion of Grenada in 1983 was intended in part to prevent the Soviets from gaining a foothold on the island. Similarly, President Johnson invaded the Dominican Republic in 1966 to keep that country from becoming another Soviet outpost in this hemisphere. Finally, and most memorably, President Kennedy contemplated a preemptive attack in the 1960s against China to prevent that nation from deploying nuclear weapons. In each of these cases, however, preemption was seen as a specific tactic to implement the policies of containment and deterrence, not as a new doctrine.

While it is one thing to favor preemption of international terrorist networks, it is quite another to suggest preempting established nation-states, even so-called rogue states. September 11 did not change the nature of international politics and state sovereignty. While terrorists in search of the perceived glories of martyrdom are not susceptible to the logic of deterrence, the dictators in charge of rogue regimes are a completely different story. History clearly supports the view that even the most tyrannical rulers are rational actors who wish to remain in power. These leaders know that, were they to use WMD for themselves or provide such weapons to terrorists, the response would be overwhelming. These dictators can effectively be contained by military and economic pressure applied by the United States. And even if containment were to break down, they would not be able to blackmail or intimidate their neighbors or our allies. They would undoubtedly understand that should they ever use WMD, the United States would certainly respond swiftly with overwhelming retaliatory force to assure their destruction. One of your closest advisers conveyed a similar understanding during the last presidential campaign. She noted in an article in *Foreign Affairs* in the spring of 2000 that "the first line of defense should be a clear and classical statement of deterrence—if they do acquire weapons of mass destruction, …these weapons will be unusable because any attempt to use them will bring national obliteration." In fact, the most likely scenario in which a dictator *would* use WMD against the U.S. homeland, troops, or allies is if that dictator perceived an imminent military action by the United States.

The other two components of the NSS are equally problematic. While maintaining military dominance and extending free-market democracy are laudable goals, they should not take precedence over or come at the expense of other, more important national priorities.

The proposed defense strategy outlined in the QDR requires adequate military power for its successful implementation. If that makes the United States militarily dominant, then it is a useful and necessary means to the required end. But military dominance should not be a goal in and of itself. Public statements to this effect unnecessarily make potential enemies afraid that the United States has become a revisionist power and send mixed messages to our allies that we might prefer to go it alone. Such a priority may also force this country to spend more than is necessary on defense and siphon money away from other important foreign policy activities that help to make the world safer from the forces of radicalism. In addition, there is the residual danger that if escalating defense budgets prevent the government from dealing with problems at home, the American public could grow restless and wary of the level of defense spending required for military readiness. Better to keep our international footprints to a minimum so as not to breed unnecessary ill will and resentment at home and abroad. The United States should reserve the right to act with due force and vigor, but only when absolutely necessary.

Finally, the United States should be cautious about entering the business of democracy promotion, as it will sometimes come at the expense of our most important national security interests. Throughout the Cold War, we spoke out eloquently about the importance of freedom and human rights, but we never endangered our nation's security by seeking to extend democracy to a country through power or force. In the 1950s and 1960s, when the Eastern European countries revolted against Soviet imperialism, we did not send in American troops to aid their cause because this would have produced a war in Europe with the Soviet Union that may have escalated to the use of nuclear weapons. When the Soviet Union put down the rebellions in Poland, Hungary, and Czechoslovakia with military force, we did condemn it loudly—but we stopped short of risky military involvements.

In the short term, the war on terrorism comes into direct conflict with the administration's pursuit of a human rights agenda. After September 11, we had to turn a blind eye to the lack of democracy in Pakistan and the former Soviet republics in Central Asia, not to mention the tactics of the Russian and Chinese governments in dealing with minorities in their countries. We were right to do this because we needed the help of these states in destroying al-Qaeda and the Taliban. In the Middle East, the war on terrorism—

not to mention our strategic interest in ensuring the free flow of oil—requires us to back a number of authoritarian regimes. While this is unfortunate, successful statecraft often requires us to evaluate the costs and benefits of policy trade-offs and prioritize our objectives accordingly. The United States must first respond to the existential threat posed by the terrorists and worry about all else after this challenge has been met and surmounted.

These sorts of compromises with our democratic principles are not new. During World War II, we formed an alliance with Josef Stalin's Soviet Union to fight the Axis powers. Similarly, during the Cold War, we had to cooperate with communist China and the military governments in Taiwan, South Korea, Greece, Turkey, Chile, and Argentina in order to contain Soviet expansionism. In hindsight, we were probably too willing to be uncomfortable bedfellows with repressive regimes during the Cold War, but ultimately, our single-minded approach to fighting the Soviets helped ensure that this struggle ended in a complete victory for the United States without a single shot being fired. Today, the path to peace and prosperity similarly lies in keeping our national priorities straight by pursuing the war on terrorism with the same hard-boiled focus and clarity of purpose that proved so successful during the Cold War.

Advantages

- Keeps the focus where it should be: fighting the global terrorist networks that pose a threat to our way of life and very existence.

- Maintains the traditional, tried-and-true approach of dealing with aggressive nation-states in the international system through containment and deterrence.

- Avoids the dangers of "imperial overstretch" and American empire-building.

- Deals with the world as it is rather than as it ought to be.

- Will be supported by our allies and even our strategic competitors, a number of whom think in like terms and so will understand

and respect this approach rather than be motivated to try to balance American power.

Disadvantages

- Risks another September 11 if this strategy's proponents underestimate the nature of the threat and wait until it is too late to respond.

- Increases the probability that tyrants who rule rogue states will acquire nuclear weapons, which they may use, provide to terrorists, or employ as tools of blackmail and coercion.

- Projects an image of weakness or lack of resolve to foes who misapprehend the nature of this strategy.

- Fails to deal with the root causes of terrorism by allowing authoritarian regimes with inept economic and backward social policies to remain in power.

- Sacrifices promotion of freedom and individual rights abroad to the war on terrorism.

Political Impact

- In Congress, this approach will be supported by traditional realists on the Senate Foreign Relations Committee and the House International Affairs Committee. Hawks and neoconservatives will oppose this approach as a relic of the Cold War.

- The Pentagon and the State Department will support the idea of not hastily embarking on preventive wars against other states, although Department of Defense officials might conclude that this strategy accepts too much risk. The Pentagon will be concerned about backing off from the idea of military dominance, with the ensuing implications for American troops if war breaks out and the impact on the military's slice of the budgetary pie.

- This approach will be greeted with a sigh of relief by our allies and the other great powers, many of whom harbor concerns that an enraged America may be adopting a go-it-alone strategy harkening back to the Wild West.

- The general public may support this approach, as it could be disinclined to support unilateral attacks on other nations or the creation of an American empire. But the American populace will also hold you responsible if there is another terrorist attack on the U.S. homeland or American troops or interests abroad. Also, some religious leaders and some progressive-minded segments of the public will frown on this approach's subordination of human rights.

OPTION THREE: A COOPERATIVE WORLD ORDER

Like the proponents of the other two approaches, advocates of the cooperative world order approach agree that the task at hand is to defeat the terrorists and tyrants who threaten this nation's security. They also generally concur with advocates of preventive action that this requires translating America's dominance into a peace that is lasting and durable—one that is roughly fashioned around our blueprint for national success: individual liberty, democracy, and free enterprise. The disagreement lies in the means to arrive at this shared goal.

To be sure, the recent intersection of radicalism with destructive technologies will sometimes require the United States to use its military might decisively to protect the American people and to make the world safer. Yet there are limitations on what force can accomplish—particularly when it is used unilaterally, without the support of our allies and partners. This country is best able to promote its interests and values when it consults with friends and with the institutions it itself took the lead role in creating. Although divergent national interests may make compromise difficult, the United States should use its immense power and influence to persuade—rather than coerce—other countries to sign on to its agenda.

In most cases, this means that the so-called preventive-action approach is neither the ideal nor the preferred way to transform our immense power into a global consensus in favor of our values and interests. Loose talk of "anticipatory self-defense" breeds fear and resentment among allies, partners, and institutions that we need behind us to wage the war on terrorism successfully. And if applied too broadly, this strategy is incompatible with how we order our domestic life, not to mention the binding norms of international law.

Article 51 of the UN Charter—a treaty that a U.S. president and the Senate pledged to uphold—explicitly supports the inherent right to use force in self-defense. This provision is generally interpreted as activating the right to self-defense when the threat of "armed aggression" is imminent. But the references to preemption in this administration's new strategy appear to carve out a much broader exception to the general prohibition on the use of force. For some, it suggests a newfound willingness to put American blood, treasure, and prestige on the line without first exhausting all available diplomatic alternatives. Advocates of the cooperative world order option prefer that the nation coordinate military enforcement actions through the UN, much as we did during the Persian Gulf War in 1990 and more recently tried to do in achieving the passage of UN Security Council Resolution 1441, which allowed the most comprehensive arms-inspections regime to date back into Iraq and furnished the legal basis for the subsequent coalition invasion of Iraq after that nation failed to cooperate with the inspectors as Resolution 1441 demanded.

As exemplified by these episodes, a policy promoting a cooperative world order would seek to use American power and influence to integrate other countries and institutions into arrangements consistent with U.S. interests and values. This strategy insists that America is committed to working with its allies and partners in international institutions such as the UN, NATO, the OAS, and other alliances.

This strategy also reaffirms a U.S. leadership role in organizations that spearhead the spread of free markets, such as the WTO, and that help developing countries respond to economic emergencies and pursue sustainable development, such as the World Bank and the International Monetary Fund (IMF). It appreciates the positive role that arms-control agreements such as the NPT can play in promoting our vital national interests. And it recognizes that the best way to ensure the smooth political and economic transformation of former adversaries is to enmesh them in organizations that support democratic principles. Rather than having the United States go off in search of empire, this approach emphasizes a combination of preventive diplomacy with collaborative efforts to promote universal norms that reflect the values and ideals that Americans hold dear.

If the United States strengthens its alliances and adapts international rules to new realities, it will not need to maintain a costly military dominance. It can reduce its defense budget, which is already bigger in 2003 than the military budgets of the next 20 largest spenders combined, and consider reducing its global military presence. The funds that are freed up can be applied toward the nonmilitary component of the annual foreign-affairs budget, including bilateral and multilateral foreign lending and assistance. These previously unavailable monies can help alleviate those conditions in countries that spawn radicalism, such as poverty and lawlessness, thereby making a significant long-term contribution to our national security.

In the final analysis, the neoconservatives are right that extolling the virtues of democracy and free markets worldwide should be the main long-term focus of our national security policy. But the appeal of American institutions loses some of its luster if this country is perceived as imposing its will on others rather than operating by building consensus. In the long run, a strategy promoting a cooperative world order will be most effective in transforming American primacy into a lasting peace.

Advantages

- Makes cooperation more likely in the war on terrorism and other international challenges that cannot be met alone, such as the proliferation of WMD, transnational crime, narcotics trafficking, global financial instability, infectious diseases, poverty, lawlessness, and environmental degradation.

- Increases the likelihood that the United States will not have to act alone in enforcement actions that are also in defense of its own national interests.

- Reduces the risk that America's unsurpassed military and economic power and cultural sway will produce resentment that results in countervailing coalitions among nation-states and new recruits for terrorists.

- Ensures that the United States stays true to the same values in the international arena that generations have worked to preserve and protect at home.

- Provides a more persuasive model for strategic competitors and rogue regimes to follow in respecting international norms.

- Allows the Department of Defense to reduce its budget and perhaps its global presence, making available resources for other foreign-affairs priorities as well as domestic needs.

Disadvantages

- May be perceived as subordinating the national interest to the collective will of other nations or international institutions.

- Constrains the ability of the United States to take forceful, direct action in defense of its interests at a time when its hard power is at its apex and it remains vulnerable to existential threats.

- May place our vital national security interests in the hands of sometimes ineffectual international organizations and under unenforceable treaties.

- Conveys a potential image of complacency and weakness to foes who equate multilateral diplomacy with doubt and indecision.

- Raises the ire of the Pentagon, which will resist budget reductions.

- Invites criticism from some Americans who are suspicious of remote, global institutions that for them portend a loss of national sovereignty.

Political Impact

- This option will be supported by the internationalists in Congress, the liberal segments of the public, the arms-control and international legal communities, and many elements of the media, but it will be adamantly opposed by neoconservatives and realists on Capitol Hill and in the Pentagon, as well as by most members of the foreign policy establishment.

- It will be enthusiastically supported by our NATO allies, particularly France and Germany, the other permanent members of the UN Security Council, developing nations, most bureaucrats in international institutions, and international civil society (nongovernmental organizations).

- The majority of the American people will support increased aid to underdeveloped countries and working with international organizations, if you emphasize the national security benefits of these actions. A small but vocal minority will see this as the beginning of an unelected world government that sacrifices the interests of working-class Americans to an illusory international community.

RECOMMENDATION

Convene your National Security Council (NSC) to review this memo and modify it as the NSC sees fit.

SPEECH ONE: U.S. DOMINANCE AND PREVENTIVE ACTION

A policy that replaces the Cold War concepts of deterrence and containment with preemption as the cardinal principle of American foreign policy; maintains military dominance for the foreseeable future; aggressively promotes democracy and free markets around the globe to deal with the root causes of terrorism.

Members of Congress and My Fellow Americans:

Thank you for welcoming me to Capitol Hill this evening. I have decided to speak directly to this joint session of Congress because our Constitution gives the president primary responsibility for conducting the foreign affairs of the nation and the 1986 Goldwater-Nichols Department of Defense Reorganization Act mandates that the president present, on an annual basis, a national security strategy to the Congress and the American people. As you know, I sent my administration's National Security Strategy to you on September 20, 2002. Since that time, however, there has been a great deal of controversy and discussion at home and around the world about the exact meaning of some of the ideas contained in the strategy and how they fit together. My purpose tonight is to clarify for you and the American people the meaning of the concepts and to gain your support for putting these ideas into practice.

The terrorist attacks of September 11, 2001, made it clear that this nation's existing national security strategy was outdated. For the last half of the twentieth century, the United States relied on a strategy of deterrence and containment to protect its vital interests, and this strategy worked exceedingly well. By demonstrating to the Soviet Union, from the end of World War II through its dissolution in 1991, that this nation and our allies had sufficient military power and were willing to use it, we prevented the Soviets from expanding their empire beyond the areas they occupied at the end of World War II. This power and will were most vividly demonstrated during the Cuban missile crisis in 1962, when together they caused the Soviet Union to remove its nuclear-tipped missiles from that island nation only 90 miles from our shores. Our military power and our willingness to use it also forced the Soviets to back down several times from trying to exert control over all of Berlin and from extending their influence into Central America and elsewhere around the world.

Although we never engaged with Soviet military forces directly during the Cold War, this triumph was not achieved without a large sacrifice of blood and treasure by the American people, particularly those 26 million volunteers and draftees who served in the armed forces from 1945 to 1990. During the 45 years that this nation waged the Cold War, about 150,000 American servicemen and servicewomen made the ultimate sacrifice. Approximately 100,000 gave their lives in the struggles against Soviet-supported surrogates in Korea and Vietnam. Another 50,000 military personnel were killed in smaller operations in places such as Lebanon, Grenada, and the Dominican Republic, or in accidents as they trained to achieve and maintain the readiness that was necessary to convince the Soviets that we could guard and retaliate against any military aggression on their part. On average, about 1,000 American military personnel died each year during the Cold War on what the Pentagon called "routine training missions."

The material cost of the Cold War was also substantial. Measured in today's dollars, our nation spent about $15 trillion, or 6 percent of our gross domestic product, on national security to win the Cold War. Not only did large expenditures on national security prevent us from dealing with some problems at home, they were responsible for saddling our children and grandchildren with more than $2 trillion in debt. But no one would argue that this sacrifice of U.S. blood and treasure was in vain. In fact the victory over the Soviet Union reaped a peace dividend that enabled us to eliminate federal budget deficits in the late 1990s.

A DECADE OF NEGLECT

From the fall of the Berlin Wall in 1989 to the collapse of the World Trade Center towers in 2001, however, there was a strategic pause in this nation. Some argued that the United States did not need a new strategic doctrine because the end of the Cold War marked the "end of history." In this view, the collapse of the Soviet empire presaged the triumph of liberal democratic capitalism, which would be the final form of human government. Therefore, the United States could just sit back and let the self-sustaining momentum of this tidal wave of liberalism crash onto foreign shores. The previous administration's National Security Strategy, which was released in December 1999, noted that the purpose of our national security was to promote security, prosperity, democracy, and human rights. But perhaps still susceptible to the logic of the "end of history" thesis, the administration that released that strategic document neglected to set forth any specific means to accomplish those lofty goals; instead, it focused on how to employ our armed forces to support humanitarian interests after a full-blown crisis had erupted.

Others argued that because of the inexorable processes of globalization, the world was becoming so interconnected that wars between nation-states were a thing of the past. They felt that the fall of communism, the rise of a global market economy, and exciting new technologies were creating not only a new economy but a "new world order." Or, to put it more directly, the discipline of the capital markets, which create vast capital flows of over a trillion dollars each year, served as a sort of global police force. The "electronic herd" of foreign investors rewarded only those countries with sound political systems, robust regulatory frameworks, and a healthy respect for the rule of law. As one pundit noted, nations with McDonald's restaurants do not go to war with each other. In essence, this camp contended that geoeconomics had replaced geopolitics, and so the United States needed to focus its efforts on enhancing its economic rather than its military power.

Still others argued that the main threats to international peace and stability were the humanitarian problems caused by "failed" states. Therefore, the primary job of the international community was to grapple with these humanitarian problems and remove their systemic causes so that these crises would not reoccur. Although the proponents of this view were later vindicated to some degree, many of them were too fixated on transforming our military from a legion of war-fighters to a team of peacekeepers.

September 11 showed these ideas to be misguided. Looking back, it is clear that the last decade was, from a national security perspective, a decade of neglect, or as some have called it, a "holiday from history." We convinced ourselves that the rising tide of economic prosperity would go on indefinitely and that no threat to our security could arise now that the Soviet bear had been defeated. We did not seek to adapt our existing alliances to potential new dangers, and when periodic regional hot spots flared up, our response was weak and indecisive, betraying our lack of resolve. Predictably, periodic cruise-missile strikes and willy-nilly interventions yielded little or no positive effect, except to build foreign animosity without incapacitating the threat.

Not only did we fail to develop a new strategic doctrine to deal with the post–Cold War world, we allowed our military power to atrophy. Not only did we reduce the size of our military too quickly, we did not even provide our men and women in uniform with the funds to replace their worn-out equipment. We allowed their combat skills to decay by turning them into peacekeepers rather than war-fighters. Not surprisingly, the morale of our fighting men and women declined as a result of playing "kindergarten cop." In the 1990s, our troops were sent off on one humanitarian mission or another once every nine weeks. Meanwhile, at home, defense spending slowed to a trickle, and many military people were forced to go on food stamps.

While our armed forces were running around on humanitarian missions, we managed to lose sight of the real, gathering danger. Our response to global terrorism during most of the past decade hardly inspired fear in this enemy. One cannot help wondering whether Osama bin Laden could have been prevented from masterminding the bloody attacks of September 11 had this country done more than lob a few cruise missiles his way back in

1998. Our policy toward outlaw states has been equally flaccid and ineffectual. In fact, the last administration downgraded the threat posed by the terrorists and tyrants who rule outlaw nations, choosing to refer to them as "states of concern" rather than denouncing them to be "rogue" regimes. In these momentous times, the very same pariahs loom larger and pose a greater threat to American interests than ever before.

Finally, our military was not compelled to take proper advantage of the revolution in military affairs to transform the armed services from a Cold War–style fighting force to one capable of meeting the challenges of the 21st century. During most of the 1990s, the military was still fighting the last war, with a mindset of fielding a mass army capable of winning a big conventional campaign. But unlike Saddam Hussein, most enemies will not be so obliging as to fight us on our own terms. Indeed, the most devastating attack on American soil—the September 11, 2001, airline hijackings—was perpetrated by a band of angry young men armed with box cutters and knives—not the type of foes the military establishment has been assiduously preparing for until recently. With these myriad problems, it is no wonder that recruiting and retention in the armed forces suffered during this decade of neglect.

At the same time that our military power atrophied, the federal government also allowed the intelligence community to decay. Not only was the Central Intelligence Agency starved for funds, it was also shackled by so many bureaucratic obstacles that it was unable to gather the human intelligence that is necessary to deal with shadowy terrorists who wish us ill.

We also did not grasp the fact that, as evil as the Soviet empire was, it had become a status quo power by the 1980s and therefore kept its allies and surrogates from supporting terrorism or buying or building weapons of mass destruction. In addition, the Soviet Union at that time had the resources to place its own nuclear weapons under tight control. With the fall of communism, those restraints were lifted and the burden of combating terrorism and the spread of weapons of mass destruction fell squarely on the United States. We found ourselves in a unipolar universe, yet we failed to fill the resulting power vacuum and take the necessary steps to ensure a peaceful transition to the new international system. We did not recognize the new realities until it was too late. We essentially ignored the 1993 attack on the World Trade Center, the 1996 attacks on our military barracks in Saudi Arabia, the 1998 attacks on our embassies in East Africa, and the 2000 attack on the USS *Cole*. I promise the American people that we will not ignore such attacks any longer.

A NEW NATIONAL SECURITY DOCTRINE

Ladies and gentlemen, the decade of neglect of our national security is now over. We have a new doctrine that I call "U.S. dominance and preventive action." It reflects a willingness to use military force, in anticipation of threats and alone, if necessary, to make the world safer for all freedom-loving peoples. As the events of September 11 vividly demonstrated, these terrorists and the tyrants who support them cannot be deterred or contained. We are at war with terrorists around the globe, with the nations that harbor them, and with those rogue regimes that not only practice and support terrorism, but also show no compunction about using or trafficking in weapons of mass destruction. To put it bluntly, we are fighting World War IV.

We will make no distinction between terrorists and those who knowingly harbor them or provide aid to them. In my view, it is impossible to distinguish between al-Qaeda and those who aid their cause. Not only will we continue to go after al-Qaeda and their terrorist brethren, we will also go after states that provide them safe haven and support. A number of these outlaw regimes are also making every attempt to acquire weapons of mass destruction. They will not be swayed even by the threat of massive retaliation. They are willing to expend all their resources, even their own lives, to achieve their goals. We cannot afford to sit idly by and allow this lethal cocktail of radicalism and technology to spill into our homeland or the homelands of our allies.

We cannot and will not wait until the terrorists or tyrants strike again. The next attack on the United States is likely to be conducted with nuclear, biological, or chemical weapons, ones we appropriately refer to as "weapons of mass destruction." To put it bluntly, we cannot defend America and our interests merely by wishful thinking. As Vice President Cheney noted, "There's no treaty [that] can solve this problem. There's no peace agreement, no policy of containment or deterrence that works to deal with this threat." And I will not sit and watch as the threat draws closer and closer. The United States of America will not permit the world's most dangerous regimes to threaten us with the world's most destructive weapons. Any outlaw regime that has ties to terrorist groups and seeks or possesses weapons of mass destruction is a grave danger to the civilized world and will be confronted.

I do not mean to scare you, but here is the reality: If the events of September 11 can be compared to Pearl Harbor, the appropriate analogy for the destruction visited by the next terrorist attack may well be Hiroshima or Nagasaki. Instead of 3,000 deaths, we might have 300,000 or 3 million, according to some government estimates. The security environment we are entering is the most dangerous the world has ever known. The margin of error we once enjoyed no longer exists. And as I noted in August 2002, there is no telling how many wars it will take to secure freedom in the homeland. But we are prepared for "the burden of long, twilight struggle," to borrow President Kennedy's phrase.

At the same time, we also cannot wait until these rogue nations acquire weapons of mass destruction, particularly nuclear weapons. Possession of such weapons would not only enable these tyrants to threaten their neighbors, it would also allow them the opportunity to provide these weapons to other rogue nations or terrorists who would relish the prospect of using them against us. Moreover, if we wait until tyrants acquire these weapons, we will find it difficult, if not impossible, to take preventive action against them. As the Cold War taught us, deterrence is a two-way street. But given the irrationality of today's enemies, it may become one-way if they should get their hands on the ultimate weapon. Because Iraq not only provided haven and support for terrorists, but also demonstrated a desire to acquire weapons of mass destruction, we had to lead a coalition to change the Iraqi regime.

The rest of the world should know that Americans are not alone in this struggle. The bombings in Bali on October 12, 2002, which killed some 200 people, illustrate that all freedom-loving peoples are at risk from terrorism. And I say this again to other nations around the world: You are either with us or with the enemy in this war. You must choose which side you are on. We will answer threats to our security, and we will defend the peace.

RESPONDING TO ARGUMENTS AGAINST PREVENTIVE ACTION

There are those who will argue that preemption is un-American and out of step with our tradition of not striking the first blow. Even a cursory reading of American history will show that this is not the case. Although anticipatory use of force is not the historical norm, it has happened far more often than many critics are willing to acknowledge. Back in 1848, President Polk launched what amounted to a preemptive attack against perceived Mexican forays onto American soil; President McKinley acted preemptively in the Spanish-American War of 1898 to end the brutal, destabilizing rule of Spain in Cuba. Although in both instances, those American presidents may have relied on convenient casus belli, neither saw it as appropriate for us to be attacked first before we used force in defense of our strategic and moral goals.

In more recent times, several of my predecessors employed this same tactic. Preventive-war thinking was a staple of the Cold War. Senior U.S. military advisers in both the Truman and the Eisenhower administrations advocated preventive-war options. Moreover, President Kennedy contemplated a preemptive strike against communist China in the early 1960s to prevent that nation from developing nuclear weapons. The Kennedy administration also pursued this "better now than later" logic in its Bay of Pigs operation in 1961. President Kennedy reaffirmed the right to anticipatory self-defense in 1962 when he authorized a naval quarantine during the Cuban missile crisis. Although he did not opt for an air strike or an invasion of Cuba, his choice of a quarantine also posed a grave danger of touching off another world war. Kennedy's successor,

President Johnson, authorized the invasion of the Dominican Republic in 1966 to prevent communism from taking hold in that nation.

President Reagan's invasion of Grenada in 1983 and his attack on Libya in 1986 could also easily be construed as preemptive strikes. The former was primarily designed to prevent the Soviets from making use of an airfield being constructed in Grenada, while the latter was intended to send a harsh message to Libya that future acts of terrorism, like the Berlin discotheque bombing that killed several American service members, would not be taken lightly.

In 1994, my immediate predecessor, President Clinton, was actually in the final stages of planning to launch a preemptive strike against the Yongbyon nuclear reactor in North Korea before former President Carter negotiated the Agreed Framework. These plans were the logical outgrowth of the Pentagon's Counter Proliferation Initiative (CPI), created in 1993. According to then secretary of defense, Les Aspin, the initiative was a necessary response to a number of radical regimes that appeared on the verge of acquiring weapons of mass destruction, in particular, Iraq and North Korea. According to Aspin, the CPI would assist in providing the United States with the capability "to deal with a Saddam Hussein with nukes." Aspin's successor in the Pentagon, William Perry, emphasized this point in a speech given in 1995 when he noted correctly that future terrorists or rogue regimes "may not buy into our deterrence theory. Indeed they may be madder than MAD [mutually assured destruction]."

Recent history also tells us that preventive war has been a legitimate strategy for many nations. In 1967, Israel saved itself from being driven into the sea by preempting the Arab armies amassing on its borders. In 1981, Israel saved the Middle East and even the world from a nuclear Armageddon when it preemptively destroyed the Iraqi nuclear facility at Osirak. Would not the world have been spared much grief and suffering if the United Kingdom and France had taken similar preventive action against Adolf Hitler in the mid-1930s when they possessed the military superiority to do so? Or if the United States had followed Winston Churchill's advice and taken preventive action against the Soviet Union in the late 1940s before it developed an atomic bomb? Or if President Kennedy's Bay of Pigs operation in 1961 had succeeded in overthrowing the tyrannical regime of Fidel Castro?

For centuries, international law has accepted that a state need not suffer an attack before it can lawfully take action to repel an imminent danger. Legal scholars condition the first use of force on the presence of an imminent threat. We need to adapt this imminence requirement to today's realities. The terrorists and tyrants that inhabit the globe will not use conventional means, such as armies, navies, and air forces, to attack us. They plan to rely on "asymmetric warfare"—the use of terror tactics and perhaps even weapons of mass destruction, weapons that will be carefully concealed, secretly delivered, and employed without warning. In this new threat environment, the inherent right to self-defense enshrined in Article 51 of the UN Charter includes the right—I would say the legal and moral obligation—to act to protect American interests. To conclude otherwise would be to turn the charter into a suicide pact.

In a perfect world, preventive action would be unnecessary. But in the admittedly flawed world of today, it is not enough to act only in response to past aggression. Even a number of "just war" theorists understand that such a reactive strategy plays into the hands of Osama bin Laden and his sympathizers. I agree with many of our religious and moral leaders who say that war should be fought only as a last resort, but preventive action is plainly defensive when it is motivated by a reasonable belief that a serial aggressor, such as Saddam Hussein's Iraq, is equipping itself with the means to carry out further aggression.

The doctrine of U.S dominance and preventive action will not be used as a license to intervene haphazardly in the affairs of other sovereign nation-states. This country has long respected the principle of non-intervention established by the 1648 Treaty of Westphalia. Even while its signatories have repeatedly compromised the sovereignty of their neighbors, the United States has almost always respected the territorial boundaries of other countries.

Yet, in recent times, international law has evolved to recognize a countervailing principle that qualifies the norm of non-intervention: regimes may surrender the right to rule over their people if they systematically deviate from established international human rights standards and consistently pose a threat to regional and global peace and stability. A state that condones or practices terrorism, or seeks to use weapons of mass destruction as weapons of choice, or retains its hold on power by violating virtually every norm of morality and law known to mankind forfeits its claim to sovereignty. This principle of forceful action for humanitarian ends was openly espoused by the last administration and its European allies when NATO intervened in Kosovo without UN authorization to stop the latest round of genocide and ethnic cleansing in the Balkans. And it applies with equal force to the rogue regimes that we must contend with today.

We have bipartisan support in favor of my position that preemption is now a necessary component of an effective defense. Democrats such as former President Clinton and Senator Joseph Lieberman, as well as Republicans such as Senator John McCain, all support this view. For example, in 1998, the former president argued that Saddam Hussein's quest to dominate the Middle East by acquiring weapons of mass destruction was an active threat to U.S. allies and interests. Senator Lieberman noted that every day Saddam remained in power was a day of danger for the Iraqi people, for Iraq's neighbors, for the American people, and for the world. Senator McCain was even more direct: he said that Saddam Hussein posed a clear and present danger to the American people.

No one should view this doctrine as an open invitation to launch aggressive wars under the pretense of self-defense. We will preempt only when we have good reason to conclude that a foe plans to attack us in the near future. Anticipatory action is a tool of last resort to be used after all diplomatic efforts have been exhausted. But it is no longer justifiable to wait until the hour of danger is upon us. History will view us harshly if we neglect our responsibilities in spite of our awesome ability to help the world become a better, safer place. President Theodore Roosevelt said it best: "A nation's first duty is within its borders, but it is not thereby absolved from facing its duties in the world as a whole; and if it refuses to do so, it merely forfeits its right to struggle for a place among the people that shape the destiny of mankind."

Some who agree that preventive war is legally and morally justifiable contend that we must be wary of taking military action unilaterally, because to do so would undermine collective-security organizations, such as the UN and NATO. They argue that we should employ military power only with UN authorization, as we did in the Persian Gulf in 1991 and in Bosnia in 1995, or with NATO authorization, as we did in Kosovo in 1999. We will certainly consult with and even try to work problems through international institutions, but we will not surrender our security to these organizations because too often they are unable or unwilling to take the decisive action necessary to protect American interests. As I insisted in my 2003 State of the Union address, "the course of this nation does not depend on the decisions of others."

For a number of years we watched the UN and our European allies struggle to bring the situation in Bosnia under control, but as they dawdled and we observed from the sidelines, the situation gravely deteriorated. Thousands died unnecessarily and hundreds of thousands more became refugees virtually overnight. The horror show ended with the Dayton Accords only after the United States entered the fray and orchestrated a NATO bombing campaign that brought the Serbs to the bargaining table. Similarly, it took over two months of aerial bombardment to drive the Serbs from Kosovo because we had to allow that war to be directed by a committee of nineteen NATO nations, all with different interests, agendas, and military capabilities.

Contrast these two episodes with the way we handled the situations in Afghanistan and Iraq. The United States led a "coalition of the willing" that brought about regime change in each of those nations in approximately a month without incurring significant casualties. These struggles not only made it difficult for al-Qaeda to attack hard targets like military or government favorites, but they toppled two of the most repressive regimes in the world. They also restored freedom and dignity to the peoples of Afghanistan and Iraq. While we prefer to reach a consensus in support of our actions, we will not let an illusory international community undermine the legitimate security concerns of this great nation. Secretary of Defense Donald Rumsfeld put it well when he said, "It is less important to have unanimity than it is to be making the right decision and doing the right thing, even though at the outset it may seem lonesome."

And as the situations in Iraq and North Korea show, diplomacy alone does not work with tyrants who have weapons of mass destruction. Throughout the 1990s, Saddam Hussein frequently violated the agreements he had made at the end of the Persian Gulf War to destroy all his weapons of mass destruction and long-range delivery systems. Despite sixteen UN resolutions, seven years of inspections, and a visit by the UN secretary-general, Iraq still maintained large quantities of biological and chemical weapons and continued to attempt to develop nuclear weapons. Even threats of regime change and cruise-missile attacks were not enough to change Saddam's behavior. It was only when we threatened him with a preemptive attack that would lead to regime change that he began even passively cooperating with inspectors. The UN Security Council had an opportunity to reassert its relevance to international politics and restore its credibility. But it failed the test. Yet even as the United Nations and some of our friends and partners shied away from the task of disarming Saddam, we led a coalition of the willing that did just that.

The situation with North Korea is equally disturbing. In 1994 the international community rewarded Pyongyang for freezing its illegal activities at Yongbyon by offering that loathsome regime two new nuclear reactors and free oil. Five years later, when evidence emerged that North Korea might have been cheating on the 1994 Agreed Framework, we offered 600,000 tons of food aid just to be able to inspect one site. What did these negotiations and de facto ransom payments get us? We now know that North Korea began systematically cheating on the 1994 Agreed Framework almost before the ink on it was dry. And, as I speak today, it may already possess a couple of nuclear weapons and is aggressively pursuing uranium- and plutonium-enrichment activities to build additional ones.

We prefer to resolve tensions on the Korean Peninsula by allowing the United Nations to negotiate a durable disarmament program. But Kim Jong Il must know that his days of extracting concessions in return for minimal cooperation are over. One way or another, like Saddam Hussein, he will soon discover that by pursuing nuclear weapons and by exporting destructive technologies abroad, he is leading his country down a path toward national ruin.

THE NEED FOR MILITARY DOMINANCE

A strategy of preemptive war alone will not be enough to win this war against terrorism and its "axis of evil" supporters. We must do much more. First, we need to maintain our conventional and nuclear military superiority and keep hundreds of thousands of troops deployed around the world for the foreseeable future. Whether we like it or not, the American military has become the ultimate guarantor of international peace and stability. We may not be the world's sheriff, but the "911" emergency calls are nevertheless routed to us. Military dominance will not only allow us to wage successful military campaigns with a minimal loss of life, as we did in Afghanistan and Iraq and may have to do in North Korea, it will also prevent any nation from undertaking a military buildup to challenge the United States.

For example, as China's economy continues to grow, that nation may be tempted to build up its military capabilities to rival ours. We cannot let that happen. A China whose military capability equals or surpasses ours will be able to dominate Northeast and Southeast Asia and thus undermine our interests in those regions. A militarily powerful China will make it difficult for us to preserve our commitments to Taiwan, Japan, and South Korea. It would also make it more challenging for us to press our human rights agenda with Beijing and would make cooperation on weapons proliferation matters less likely.

By continuing to modernize our military as we have done these past few years, and by keeping up our military presence around the globe, we can demonstrate to China and any other nation that hopes to rival us that they simply cannot catch us no matter how much they spend. And by making any arms race futile, the United States will have helped maintain a peaceful, stable world free of great-power rivalry.

The secretary of defense put it well when he noted in January 2002, "Our goal is not simply to fight and win wars. It is to prevent wars. To do so, we need to find ways to influence the decision-makers of our potential adversaries, to deter them not only from using existing weapons, but to the extent possible, try to dissuade them from building dangerous new capacities in the first place."

Some might argue that maintaining military dominance will be too great a drain on our resources. That is simply not true. Thanks to the tremendous performance of our economy, we have achieved our present military superiority at a cost of only 3 percent of our gross domestic product. This is about half of what we spent, on average, in the Cold War or during the Reagan administration. Similarly, at the height of its imperial reign, from 1870 to 1913, the United Kingdom spent an average of 3.1 percent of its GDP on defense. As long as we continue to put at least 3 percent of our GDP into defense and continue to transform our military, we should be able to maintain this dominance. If China or any other nation attempts to challenge us militarily we can easily add another 1 percent of GDP, or $100 billion, to our annual defense budget, without disrupting our economy or neglecting legitimate social needs. Moreover, the cost to our economy from another terrorist attack, especially one with weapons of mass destruction, will be far greater than 1 percent of our GDP. The costs to our economy from the attacks of September 11 have already exceeded $200 billion.

Some have argued that instead of hard military power, the United States should rely more on "soft power" to exert its influence. Proponents of this view, which was most famously asserted by Harvard political scientist Joseph Nye, contend that nontraditional components of a nation's power such as its cultural sway, the strength of its ideas, and the quality of its commercial goods can exert influence in world affairs. While this idea sounds great in theory, it does not work in practice. Many of those who hate us most eat at McDonald's, drink Coke or Pepsi, listen to American CDs, and watch DVDs of Hollywood movies. As the British discovered in the nineteenth century, nationalist movements paradoxically sprang up among indigenous populations in the most Anglicized parts of the British Empire.

THE NEED TO EXTEND DEMOCRACY

Finally, preempting our enemies and maintaining military dominance, while necessary to winning the war against terrorism, are not alone sufficient to ensure our victory. To be successful in this endeavor we must aggressively seek to extend democracy throughout the globe. The events of September 11 have shown us that it is authoritarian or totalitarian governments that spawn, promote, and harbor terrorist movements. The recent report on Arab Human Development by the United Nations noted that the Arab states have fallen so far behind the rest of the world in economic terms that their combined GDP does not equal even that of Spain. According to the UN report, this poor economic performance is attributable to an overall lack of freedom, modern education systems, and respect for women's rights.

It is clear that if we do not spread democratic values to these Arab states, even if doing so would mean using military force, conditions will continue to deteriorate both absolutely and in relation to the rest of the world. We know that democratic governments will, among other things, help build more open and productive economies, empower women, and create a free press that will educate and inform citizens as well as hold the governments accountable for failed policies. Creating these conditions should reduce significantly the supply of terrorists like the ones who attacked us on September 11.

I know that some will argue that this is naïve Wilsonian idealism or empire-building in disguise. I could not disagree more. Given the events of September 11, this is the only realistic choice we have left. In this new era we cannot have stability without broadening the community of democratic nations with open markets. Moreover, the values that we are attempting to spread are universal values, not American values. As I mentioned in my State of the Union address, they are God's gift to humanity, not the American people's gift to the world.

We do not seek to establish an empire. As I have said on several occasions since assuming office, America has no empire to extend or utopia to establish. We are committed to freedom for ourselves and for others so that everywhere people are able to pursue their lives' ambitions free of fear. But this liberty will prove illusory without American military and economic power first securing the peace and then setting into motion a stable transition to more open societies.

PREEMPTION, DOMINANCE, AND THE EXTENSION OF DEMOCRACY GO TOGETHER

Others will disagree and argue that a doctrine of preemption alone will be enough to win this war against terrorism. They will say we do not need to have military dominance or to aggressively promote democracy on every continent. This perspective is shortsighted and unduly cautious. My grand strategy is a three-legged stool. Without military dominance we cannot take preemptive action successfully or keep rival great-power aspirations at bay. Moreover, if we abandon the challenge of extending democracy to every corner of the globe, we will never address the root causes of terrorism, no matter how many preemptive campaigns we wage or how militarily dominant we are and appear to be.

I understand that this new grand strategy will be viewed by some of you as too bold or too burdensome. Indeed, many said the same thing back in 1945, as World War II was coming to a close. Eschewing the advice of the diffident and the indecisive, the United States conquered and reconstructed Germany and Japan, making sure those countries would never threaten the world again by helping transform them into free-market democracies. More than half a century later, this great nation once again prepares to embark on a bold plan to reshape another region tainted by unspeakable evil. If we succeed in transforming Iraq, the most malignant Arab state, into a democracy then we will be able to usher the entire Middle East into a new, more progressive era. We will act in the spirit of Presidents Roosevelt and Truman and temper our justice with mercy, reforming the most dangerous of outlaw nations that ignore the call of history, while displaying generosity without a trace of vindictiveness when the enemy is defeated. Given the events of September 11, the United States must take bold actions as the world's leading military and economic power. Our moment to act is now, while our strength is unparalleled and our enemies are on the run. To be sure, I know my audacious vision is not without danger. But the cost of continuing to pursue the reactive policies of containment and deterrence will be far greater in the long run than any short-term risks we might incur in implementing all aspects of a preventive-action strategy. Better to confront the danger now than to wait until it is too risky or simply too late to act. Accordingly, I seek your support for all aspects of my bold, new defense strategy of U.S. dominance and preventive action. As President Reagan noted in devising his visionary approach that brought down the Soviet empire, "If not now, when; if not us, who?"

SPEECH TWO: A MORE STABLE WORLD WITH U.S. POWER FOR DETERRENCE AND CONTAINMENT

A traditional balance-of-power approach to national security in which preemption may be employed as a tactic but should not be elevated to the status of a strategy; emphasizes that robust containment and active deterrence still work, even in dealing with rogue states or the tyrants who rule them, especially when used in conjunction with international support; recognizes that nations do not have permanent friends or enemies but rather permanent interests; opposes broadening the core of vital national interest to include eliminating all forms of terrorism and all varieties of evil; remains skeptical of the prospects of exporting democracy worldwide, but particularly in the Middle East; and views stability over the promotion of democracy as the primary aim of international politics.

Members of Congress and My Fellow Americans:

I have decided to speak to you tonight to make clear what my new National Security Strategy really means and how it will be implemented. As you know, since I forwarded that strategy to you in September 2002, there has been a great deal of controversy and confusion over the strategy's specific implementation. Public officials and pundits here and around the world have quoted selectively from that document to endorse or criticize the strategy. It is certainly true that the attacks of September 11, 2001, were a shock to this nation. But these attacks did not fundamentally alter the nature of international politics or the existential threats to our security. There is nothing really new about actions by terrorists against the United States, its interests, and its allies. In the past decade alone, we were attacked several times, although none rivaled the scale of devastation felt on September 11.

As you well know, the World Trade Center was attacked by terrorists for the first time on February 26, 1993. Those extremists used a car bomb that killed six Americans, injured more than a thousand, and caused $600 million in damage. In June 1996, terrorists attacked the al-Khobar Towers complex at a U.S. air base in Saudi Arabia, which housed thousands of U.S. servicemen and servicewomen supporting the planes that patrolled the southern no-fly zone in Iraq. These cowardly attacks killed nineteen of our brave military personnel and wounded scores of others. Two years later, al-Qaeda terrorists blew up our embassies in Kenya and Tanzania, slaughtering twelve Americans and more than 200 innocent citizens of those East African nations. And in May of 2000, terrorists supported by al-Qaeda attacked the USS *Cole*, killing seventeen of our courageous sailors and wounding dozens of others.

So this threat has existed for some time; the real problem lies in how we responded to those incidents. Instead of going after the perpetrators of these craven acts with the full force of American power, we contented ourselves with a strategy of accommodation, half-measures, and wishful thinking. Our indecision sent a clear message to al-Qaeda that we did not take these threats seriously. We moved reluctantly despite the fact that after the bombings of the two American embassies in East Africa in 1998, the director of central intelligence told the intelligence community that he considered the country to be at war against this dangerous terrorist network. And we compounded the problem by relying on legal technicalities as an excuse not to take Osama bin Laden into custody, even though the government of Sudan offered to hand him over to us in 1996. Indeed, one has to wonder if the events of September 11 could have been averted had this country not abandoned Afghanistan to its own devices in the late 1980s or had the U.S. government responded with greater vigor to the series of terror attacks perpetrated by al-Qaeda against American interests over the last several years.

Despite several warnings by high-level groups, we also refused to beef up our security at home—or, as we now refer to it, to enhance our homeland security. But a number of experts made clear that the handwriting for a catastrophe was on the wall. In 1997, the Pentagon's Quadrennial Defense Review listed homeland defense first among vital U.S. interests, as it concluded that the Department of Defense must sustain and improve U.S. counterterrorism capabilities. That same year, the National Defense Panel, which was chartered by Congress to evaluate the Quadrennial Defense Review and to produce an independent assessment from outside the Pentagon, came to a similar conclusion. That panel argued that homeland defense was the first area that needed to be addressed in meeting national security challenges in the 21st century and stated that homeland defense should include not only a shield against ballistic missile attacks but also defenses against terrorism, information warfare, and weapons of mass destruction delivered by means other than ballistic missiles.

Similarly, in its first report in September 1999 and its final one in February 2001, the National Security Strategy Group (often referred to as the Hart-Rudman Commission) rather prophetically warned that this nation would see a far more insidious form of violence in the 21st century: catastrophic terrorism. It grimly concluded that in the first two decades of the 21st century large numbers of Americans would die on our home soil. Finally, in February 2001, some six months before the attacks of September 11, the director of the Defense Intelligence Agency, Admiral Thomas Wilson, told Congress that over the next twelve to fourteen months he feared "a major terrorist attack against United States interests, whether here or abroad, perhaps with a weapon designed to produce mass casualties." The nation's policymakers were warned of this mounting threat, but they failed to take appropriate action to secure the homeland.

DETERRENCE AND CONTAINMENT

The time has come for a clear-eyed, hard-nosed assessment of the capabilities and limitations of American power. The United States should not squander its moment of primacy by overestimating its ability to impose its will on others without creating unforeseeable future dangers. At the same time, this country cannot rely excessively on international institutions. Peace and stability are not created by rules; they are reinforced by the residual threat of force implic-it in carefully orchestrated balances of power. Nor should the United States use September 11 as an opportunity to remake the world by somewhat naïvely and sentimentally thinking it can forcibly export democracy and free markets abroad at every turn. The country should focus on the narrower goal of defeating al-Qaeda and simultaneously use tough-minded diplomacy and a con-spicuous American force posture to deter and contain rogue states that covet weapons of mass destruction. All the while, we should never lose sight of the fact that it is better to show the velvet glove and rule with an iron fist than to overtly display the type of arro-gance that alienates needed allies and incites our foes.

Since September 11, 2001, we have declared war on terrorists with global reach and, in particular, taken long-overdue steps to crack down on al-Qaeda extremists. After the Taliban regime in Afghanistan refused to turn over Osama bin Laden and his band of terrorists, we invaded that country and overthrew one of the most horrible and repressive regimes the world has ever known, in the process chasing most of the terrorists out of their safe haven. We have done well to hunt down remnants of al-Qaeda in all corners of the globe. Although that struggle is still ongoing, we have put al-Qaeda on the defensive and have made it more difficult for its operatives to plot or carry out other attacks against our nation or our interests. While we seek to defeat all terrorists with global reach, we will continue to focus on finally ridding the world of al-Qaeda and its affiliated sympathizers.

We undertook the mission in Afghanistan in a precise and sur-gical manner so as to avoid creating the perception overseas and at home that we were acting with a heavy hand or unilaterally. The UN Security Council initially authorized the mission to go after the Taliban and al-Qaeda. It has since helped us to install an inter-im government in Afghanistan and has taken the lead in the efforts to rebuild that war-torn country. Our European allies have stepped in as well. For the first time in its over 50 years of existence, NATO invoked Article V of its charter, declaring that the attacks on the World Trade Center and the Pentagon were in effect an attack on all nineteen members of the alliance. The military occupation force that continues to provide security for Kabul and its environs is composed of troops from several nations. It has been commanded successively by British, Turkish, German, and Dutch generals and soon will come directly under the command of NATO. Our coalition partners have also taken responsibility for training the police in that country. All told, General Tommy Franks's efforts have been supported by the military contributions of some 90 nations. The war against terrorism is not just America's war, it is the world's war, and we have gone to great lengths to communicate to all nations that we are together in this struggle against a common enemy.

In the long run, we need the help of our allies to eliminate al-Qaeda cells and reduce the instability in the Middle East that breeds discontent. We are presently sharing information with law enforcement and intelligence agencies around the globe to hunt down these radicals. And we are working with our friends around the world to dry up the financial assets of these global terrorists. To date, the world community has frozen more than $100 million in terrorists' financial assets. As a result of these actions, we have preempted a number of terrorist attacks on the United States and its interests, arresting more than 3,000 of these evil-doers, in countries such as the United Kingdom, France, Italy, Jordan, Lebanon, Saudi Arabia, Spain, and Turkey, before they had the opportunity to sow more destruction.

Within our own borders, we have also made tremendous progress in preventing and deterring terrorist attacks. Thanks to the support of Congress, the Department of Homeland Security is now up and operating. Although much more needs to be done, particularly for our first responders at the state and local levels, our borders are more secure, our ports have much tighter control over what is entering and leaving, and all our modes of transportation, especially airline travel, are much safer.

As we turn to the future, our first priority must be to cement an effective strategy against terrorists and tyrants who wish us ill. But although military force will be necessary at times, it is a blunt instrument in neutralizing elusive bands of terrorists. If anything, indiscriminate military campaigns will serve only to incite hatred in parts of the world that already cast a suspicious eye on American foreign policy. For many Islamic societies, America's benign hegemony is an oxymoron. A policy of conquering, occupying, and reconstructing foreign societies will heighten resentments abroad and may inadvertently serve as fodder for terrorist propagandists in search of new recruits. And inside our own borders, the general public harbors its own doubts about an imperial agenda. We must make sure that we retain domestic support for the ongoing war on terrorism, lest we allow the home front to collapse as it did—with disastrous consequences—in the Vietnam War. This is why we will turn over control of Iraq to the Iraqi people as quickly as possible.

With these constraints in mind, the United States will focus its efforts first on tracking down and bringing to justice all members of al-Qaeda and its close affiliates, rather than dissipate its energies on fighting a global struggle against all terrorist organizations simultaneously. This campaign will emphasize diplomacy, intelligence, and secret operations over conventional military interventions. At the same time, we will pursue policies in the Islamic world that dampen the flames of anti-Americanism, which threaten to expand the cadre of future al-Qaeda recruits. The way to win the struggle against radicalism is to work aggressively to round up the terrorists while at the same time keeping a low profile so as not to draw the fire of key allies and partners in the Islamic world and elsewhere.

As I noted in my National Security Strategy, one facet of our grand strategy includes a new willingness to preempt threats with force if necessary. In the war against al-Qaeda and its brethren, deterrence alone is not enough to discourage those who seek salvation in mass murder and who cannot easily be found and punished. But military preemption will be a tool of last resort against aggressive nation-states, rather than a weapon of choice. While it sometimes has its advantages, striking first comes with serious risks as well, a point I will expand on later. I have not forgotten the Prussian statesman Otto von Bismarck's characterization of preventive war as "suicide induced by fear of death." The best way to preempt threats before they materialize is through hard-boiled diplomacy, diligent intelligence work, and efficient covert operations.

Our friends and allies understand that weapons of mass destruction in the hands of unpredictable, outlaw states represent a threat not just to the United States but to themselves as well. We will continue to work with like-minded countries on all aspects of a comprehensive strategy of robust containment and active deterrence, while recognizing that we will not always agree on the means to eradicate this threat. The global landscape is marred by several repugnant regimes, but even in the aftermath of September 11, the United States and the rest of the world can still be safe if we do not allow the scorpions to crawl out of the bottle we helped construct to contain them. In short, the appropriate strategy is to disarm dangerous regimes rather than overthrow them. This pragmatic policy of containing rogue states is now supported by most of our major allies. While some of them might be willing to join us in a coalition to remove those regimes in preventive wars, most would not. Expending scarce political capital on such military adventures will only reduce support for the critical war on terror. And we will still need assistance from our friends to defray the costs of occupying and reconstructing countries in parts of the world where we are not very familiar with local culture and traditions. This help may not be forthcoming if nations are prodded into a coalition of the sullen and unwilling.

I am confident that we do not need to wage preventive war against established nation-states. Aggressive regimes with ambitions of acquiring weapons of mass destruction can be contained and deterred as the Soviet Union was during the Cold War, even if these states obtain the ultimate weapon. They know that if they attack us or our allies, or contract out to terrorists to do their dirty work for them, they will incur massive American retaliation that would culminate in a regime change. In fact, ironically, the most likely scenario in which an outlaw regime would use catastrophic weapons against the U.S. homeland, its troops, and its allies is in the event of a preventive war intended to disarm and remove that regime from power.

The despots atop the most offensive regimes are political survivors. They understand the lessons of the recent military operation in Afghanistan that led to the ouster of the Taliban. Our quarrel was not so much with that hateful regime but with its terrorist surrogate. Had Mullah Muhammad Omar handed over Osama bin Laden, the mullah and his cronies would have stayed in power. Similarly if Saddam Hussein had destroyed his weapons of mass destruction as the UN demanded, he too would have been allowed to remain in power. These tyrants understand that if they provide destructive technologies to terrorists or assist any terrorist network in acquiring weapons of mass destruction, they should be prepared to pay the ultimate price for their bad judgment. But if a telegraphed preventive punch makes regime change a fait accompli, these rogue states can be expected to grow more accepting of risk.

Saddam Hussein was undoubtedly a menace who inflicted much pain and suffering on his people, not to mention his unfortunate neighbors. He sought to dominate the Persian Gulf, control its oil, and obtain catastrophic weapons to realize these ambitions. But for starters, there was not enough evidence linking him to terrorist organizations, much less the attacks of September 11. Unlike the terrorists' aims, Saddam's rather mundane aspirations were grounded in the material world; he did not seek the perceived glories of the afterlife found in murderous martyrdom or share the terrorists' radical vision of society. He had little reason to make common cause with al-Qaeda. But since over the past decade he had violated seventeen UN resolutions demanding that he give up his weapons of mass destruction, we had no choice but to lead a coalition of the willing to disarm him. However, once order is restored in Iraq, we will turn power over to the Iraqi people and appropriate international organizations, so that we can withdraw quickly.

As the regime in Iran shows signs of change, we will consider improving relations with that country in order to create, over time, stable equilibrium in the Middle East. This will allow U.S. armed forces eventually to play a less visible role in regional affairs.

But in the unlikely event that our disarmament diplomacy fails and deterrence no longer appears viable, the United States will be mindful of the strictures of the so-called Powell Doctrine when it takes action. We learned from the tragedy of Vietnam that if this country commits troops, it should do so wholeheartedly and with the intention of winning quickly and decisively. That episode also taught us that the president and Congress must work together to build a general consensus among the people in support of our fighting men and women's mission and that, finally, all of our deployments must have an "exit strategy" to avoid "mission creep."

This realist approach also acknowledges that sometimes we have to hold our collective noses and negotiate directly with even the most reprehensible of regimes. We are today shifting toward such a strategy vis-à-vis North Korea. In fact, a brief glance at our history with that troubled nation confirms that successive American presidents have chosen to place pragmatism over naïve principles in sitting down and talking with the North Koreans.

President Clinton opted against a preemptive strike against North Korea in 1994 in favor of a negotiated agreement in which economic inducements were used to freeze that country's nuclear weapons program. His predecessor handled this intractable situation in a similar manner. In 1989, the first President Bush discovered that the North Koreans might be violating the nuclear Nonproliferation Treaty by processing weapons-grade nuclear material. In exchange for Pyongyang's agreeing to allow the International Atomic Energy Agency to monitor and inspect North Korea's nuclear facilities, the first President Bush withdrew our nuclear weapons from South Korea, canceled a joint military exercise with South Korea, and agreed to a high-level meeting with North Korean officials. Indeed, our tradition of managing difficult issues with that regime dates back to the 1960s, when President Johnson negotiated the release of the crew of the USS *Pueblo* after it had been held in captivity for almost a year.

Likewise, all throughout the Cold War we negotiated with the Soviet Union on everything from the number of nuclear weapons each side should hold to the rules of the road for our naval vessels. We did this because, even though we loathed the Soviets' totalitarian philosophy and their disregard for human dignity, we shared the common purpose of preventing a nuclear holocaust. President Nixon's historic visit to China was another wise decision to set aside our philosophical convictions in order to serve even more important American objectives during the Cold War.

This same clear thinking should be applied to our present-day dealings with North Korea. Intelligence officials estimate that in the near future, that country may turn on a reprocessing plant that can produce weapons-grade nuclear material. In the real world, not all security threats can be definitively resolved through risky military campaigns and brinkmanship. We are right not to want to reward or accommodate a regime intent on extracting concessions through episodic violations of its commitments. But time is running out before North Korea enters the bomb-making business. Should it develop a modest-sized nuclear arsenal, our ability to exert influence over its decisions in this regard will be diminished.

The best option available is to make clear to the North Koreans that their economic and political aspirations cannot be realized if they continue to harbor nuclear ambitions. It is my hope that a diplomatic dialogue will result in a more stringent, verifiable inspections regime in North Korea that makes sure that the country is no longer a nuclear menace. But if that regime refuses direct discussions and continues along its present path, we will have no choice but to consider all available military options, including the use of nuclear weapons. As a general matter, former Secretary of Defense William Cohen was right to note that merely huffing and puffing will not blow down Kim Jong Il's house or calm North Korea's anxious neighbors.

Finally, a realistic approach to the proliferation of weapons of mass destruction requires us to acknowledge frankly that the forces of globalization make it more difficult to stanch the spread of deadly technologies and their delivery vehicles. The Pentagon's own recent analysis shows that the ranks of extant and emerging threats include no fewer than twelve nations with nuclear weapons programs, thirteen with biological weapons activities, sixteen with chemical weapons programs, and twenty-eight nations with ballistic missile activities.

Accordingly, international cooperation through the global nonproliferation regime, as well as ad hoc measures taken with other states, is the only way to restrict the supply of these catastrophic weapons. Nonproliferation initiatives are far from perfect. It can be awfully difficult to verify and enforce compliance with them, as there are always countries like Iraq and North Korea who cheat on their treaty obligations. Nonetheless, the global regime we have in place—warts and all—is still the only game in town and is worth our continued participation and involvement.

One specific proliferation concern is that a terrorist organization will obtain fissile material, or even nuclear weapons, from the former Soviet empire. Some justified the war against Iraq on the grounds that Baghdad would pass along its nuclear weapons material and know-how to al-Qaeda. It is highly unlikely that Saddam would have taken the risk of being detected in doing so. The more immediate danger is that a terrorist network will go to the far reaches of the former Soviet Union to get its hands on unsecured fissile material and unemployed nuclear scientists desperate for work. Rather than focusing our sights on a less serious threat, we should turn our attention to broadening existing Nunn-Lugar programs for the safe collection, storage, and disposal of old Soviet-era nuclear weapons.

PROBLEMS WITH PREEMPTION

Today, the adoption of preemptive strategies against known terrorist organizations is relatively uncontroversial. These groups' stealthy nature makes it difficult to threaten retaliation, and their fanatical zeal makes it less likely that deterrence would work anyway. The past practices and public remarks of terrorist groups with global reach are enough to fulfill the traditional requirement for preemptive action that the threat be imminent.

More problematic is the idea of striking first against other states, even rogue states. Elevating preemption to a doctrine with respect to rogue states, as some have done by selectively quoting from my National Security Strategy, will actually make us less secure in several ways. First, if preemption should assume the stature of a doctrine rather than just one available tactic, then the United States will undermine its credibility if it does not wage preventive war against every nation that is in the process of acquiring nuclear, biological, or chemical weapons.

The concern is that if we openly announce such an aggressive policy and demand that our allies toe the line with us, we will have effectively put ourselves in a position in which we must either undertake risky military action or place the security of allies and partners who have sided with us in jeopardy. We cannot just stir up a hornet's nest with threats of action and then allow those closest to the peril who have publicly stood with us to contend with the fallout when we think better of acting precipitously. If we do so, we will lose the trust and confidence of our friends. As the North Korean situation demonstrates, we simply are not prepared to undertake preventive war in circumstances where the risks are potentially grave, are difficult to calibrate, and place our own allies in harm's way.

Therefore, let me state once again that preemption is only one of a number of tools that we may employ to deal with threats to our security.

Second, preempting rather than containing tyrannical regimes would prevent us from keeping the necessary policy focus to win the struggle against al-Qaeda and its close affiliates, not to mention grapple effectively with a host of other threats to our national security. Against the backdrop of great uncertainty, now is not the moment for an audacious American foreign policy of launching preventive wars. Rather, we must take careful stock of the risks and opportunities before us and then go about the difficult business of prioritizing our responses to them.

Just consider briefly the daunting array of challenges the United States now faces:

- A global war against terrorism that—as the attacks in Saudi Arabia and Morocco in mid-May 2003 demonstrate—is not over, has taken on uncertain dimensions, and has continued to cost hundreds of billions of dollars.

- A nation-building operation in Afghanistan that is costing over $1 billion a month and is far from finished.

- Establishing law and order in, reconstructing, and reinventing Iraq, a non-democratic, heterogeneous Muslim state.

- A looming showdown with a nuclear-capable North Korea that, if not skillfully handled, could cause hundreds of thousands of casualties in South Korea and Japan, destabilize Northeast Asia for decades to come, and lead to the proliferation of nuclear weapons throughout the globe.

- A divided regime in Iran that may be developing its own nuclear weapons and long-range ballistic missiles with the assistance of a new American ally.

- Implementing the road map so that violence between Israel and the Palestinians is brought under control.

- An unstable South Asian subcontinent, where India and Pakistan possess the fourth- and seventh-largest armed forces in the world, respectively, and hold hundreds of nuclear weapons that could be used in anger over the disputed territory of Kashmir.

In a world so chock full of uncertainty, we must maintain our focus and pursue our objectives with strategic clarity. First and foremost, America must give priority to defeating al-Qaeda and like-minded terrorists who pose an existential threat to our way of life. All of our other priorities should be momentarily subordinated until this objective is achieved. Waging the war against second-order security threats, such as Iraq, has diverted our attention from the task at hand. The war against Iraq and its messy aftermath could increase the probability of terrorist attacks at home, create unwanted enemies in the Islamic world, tie down hundreds of thousands of American forces for decades, and eventually cost hundreds of billions of dollars.

Waging a war, even a short one, is a tremendous undertaking. Recent history teaches that doing so will necessarily divert our attention from the struggle against terrorism. We know that the federal government is chronically unable to deal with more than one conflict at a time. The previous administration's preoccupation with the bloodshed in Bosnia in part caused it to lose sight of the low-tech slaughter in Rwanda. Earlier, in the Carter administration, the Iranian hostage crisis overshadowed all other issues for over a year, including even the Soviet invasion of Afghanistan. Decades prior, but with the Cold War already in full bloom, the Eisenhower administration's prolonged focus on the Suez crisis was one reason why it stood aside as the Soviets crushed the Hungarian revolt in 1956. This abbreviated tour of recent history shows how difficult it is to handle multiple foreign policy crises at once. We can ill afford to divert our gaze from the real threat posed by terrorism and prematurely embark on preventive wars against lesser threats when tough-minded diplomacy is managing the problem.

Third, undue preoccupation with preemption as a doctrine rather than a tactic will create instability in the international system if other nations make it the cardinal principle of their own national security policies. We should not set a precedent that legitimizes the use of preemptive force in interstate relations. If we do so, we will inevitably beg the question: If the United States can assert the right to act preemptively solely based on its own judgment, why should not others be their own prosecutor, judge, and jury?

This boomerang effect could lead India to justify an attack on Pakistan because that nation allegedly supports and trains terrorists infiltrating Kashmir and because it possesses nuclear weapons. A conventional attack by India could quickly escalate to a nuclear exchange on the South Asian subcontinent. In fact, Pakistani President Pervez Musharraf reportedly told a group of Pakistani air force veterans in December 2002 that he had been prepared to use Pakistan's nuclear weapons a year earlier, if Indian troops had crossed the Line of Control in Kashmir. Similarly, one cannot rule out Pakistan's launching a preemptive strike against Indian nuclear weapons facilities during the next crisis.

Russia could justify an occupation of Georgia on the grounds that the small country has allegedly harbored separatist Chechen fighters on its territory and is moving too slowly to capture Islamic extremists tied to the war in Chechnya. Thus, while U.S. declarations are not the only influence on the behavior of other states, they may provide sufficient political cover for others to wage wars under the false pretense of self-defense. This risk is heightened in contexts where one state claims that an enemy possesses weapons of mass destruction and that immediate action is necessary to nip the threat in the bud before it is too late.

Inadvertently setting such a precedent could undermine international norms the world has developed over several hundred years to steer nations away from unnecessary wars. The line between self-defense and aggression is not always so clear, and opportunistic nations might take advantage of tensions to launch destructive wars of aggression. Remember that Adolf Hitler justified his invasion of Poland in 1939 and of the Soviet Union in 1941 on the basis of preventive war. The Japanese also claimed that their attack on Pearl Harbor was a preventive strike intended to keep America from being able to wage war on Japan. With this history in mind, it would be short-sighted to provide other countries with handy excuses for undertaking their own preemptive campaigns.

Therefore, any preventive action must be justified on the basis of a hard-headed, cost-benefit analysis of the short-term and long-term consequences of taking action. This means that the benefit of eliminating a nation's weapons of mass destruction and wiping out a ruthless regime must be weighed against the likely expenditure of American blood and treasure, the effect on the world's economy, the costs and risks inherent in rebuilding the nation, the projected impact on regional stability, the potentially adverse reaction of our allies and partners, and such a reaction's consequences for unrelated but important American objectives.

PROBLEMS WITH EXTENDING DEMOCRACY AND EMBRACING MILITARY DOMINANCE

While we would like the rest of the world to adopt our democratic ideals and cooperate with us on every issue, we know that this is not likely. As we learned early on in our history, nations do not have permanent friends or enemies, but they do have permanent interests. And when vital national interests demand forging new ties or ending old friendships, many countries feel they have no choice but to respond to the imperatives of international politics. Interests will clash, and when they do, the possibilities for cooperation are diminished.

We also know that trying to impose democracy through the barrel of a gun is likely to backfire. Such moral campaigns to remake the world are too idealistic. Often, they are not received by the beneficiaries as gifts of benevolence and generosity but are viewed as paternalistic imperialism. They touch off resentments that make enemies of those whom we seek to convert to our way of life.

Two relatively recent episodes shed light on this point. In September 1982, we sent military forces to Lebanon, where they were initially welcomed with open arms by all factions. But about a year later, after we came to the aid of the Lebanese army, a Shi'ite truck-bomber blew up the Marine Corps barracks at the Beirut airport, killing 241 American military personnel. Our experience in Somalia a decade later confirmed the cautionary lessons of Beirut. This exercise in nation-building ended in disaster. Not surprisingly, our army was ill suited to the role of playing peacekeeper in this far-flung humanitarian mission. Indeed, our precipitous withdrawal from that African nation following the tragic deaths of eighteen American soldiers in October 1993 may have emboldened Osama bin Laden to question our resolve in the face of U.S. casualties. American power is best used to deter or defeat aggression, not to do unsolicited good deeds around the world.

While we continue to support the human rights of peoples everywhere, we will take care to place our own security needs first, as all nations must. To be certain, promoting individual rights is an important part of our grand strategy. A pragmatic foreign policy recognizes, however, that sometimes this agenda runs into conflict with other, more vital security concerns. Although it may be somewhat unpalatable, in the short run we will have to make difficult compromises in order to enhance our security and make the world more peaceful in the long run.

For example, to obtain Pakistan's crucial cooperation in the war in Afghanistan, we have had to tolerate President Musharraf's repressive policies toward his people, his half-hearted attempts to reduce terrorism in Kashmir, and his threats to use nuclear weapons against India. Not to mention the fact that his regime has evidently shared sophisticated nuclear technology, warhead-design information, and data from nuclear weapons tests with North Korea and may now be doing the same for Iran. We also have had to turn a blind eye toward Yemen's purchase of Scud missiles from North Korea, since we need the former country's help in breaking up the large concentrations of al-Qaeda members staying as uninvited guests there. Similarly, as a favor to the Russians, we have placed three Chechen rebel groups on our list of terrorists, and we have had to mute our criticism of the questionable methods Russia is employing to crack down on Chechen rebels and of the suspect practices the Chinese have adopted in response to their own separatist problem and against harmless groups such as Falun Gong.

These accommodations are not new. To defeat Hitler's Germany in World War II, we formed an alliance with Josef Stalin, although the man was a tyrant who would eventually kill over twenty million of his own people. To contain the Soviet Union during the Cold War, we extended a hand at different times to communist China and to a number of military juntas scattered throughout the globe in places such as Argentina, Chile, Greece, Taiwan, and Turkey. While these episodes hardly constitute the proudest moments of our Cold War diplomacy, our ability to stay focused on the larger goal of containing communism ultimately paid dividends when the Soviet empire peacefully collapsed under the pressure of decades of security competition with the United States. A similar sense of strategic clarity will serve us well today as we fight the war on terrorism.

History also teaches us that by attempting to maintain military dominance and by seeking to forcibly extend the circle of democracies outward, the United States will in effect be signing on to the creation of an American empire in which it alone will be responsible for bringing peace and order to every point on the globe. History also tells us that global hegemony never lasts, and so this Pax Americana, too, will come to an end. Empire-builders such as the Romans, the Chinese, the Spaniards, the French, the Austro-Hungarians, and most recently the British all found that the social, economic, and military exertions required to maintain imperial dominance against all comers invariably erode the health of the very society that achieves it. Indeed, we are already the world's largest debtor nation and more dependent on foreign capital than at any time in the last 50 years. Foreign nations now have claims on the United States for approximately $8 trillion, or 80 percent of our annual GDP.

In the end, we could lose our national soul, as we almost did in Vietnam, when America tried unsuccessfully to bring democracy to that Southeast Asian nation as part of the worldwide struggle against communist expansionism. We took the logic of Soviet containment too far in the jungles of Southeast Asia, and we would be well advised not to repeat that part of our history in the present war on terrorism. When we are tempted to revive Woodrow Wilson's dream of making the world safe for democracy, we should keep in mind the prescient insight of his secretary of state, Edmund Lansing, as to the likely fate of this grand experiment. Lansing noted that while the idea of self-determination sounded great in theory, it would be disastrous if put into practice. He said, "It will raise hopes that can never be realized. It will, I fear, cost thousands of lives. In the end it is bound to be discredited, to be called the dream of an idealist who failed to realize the danger before it was too late to check those who attempt to put the principle into force."

Millions of young lives would soon be extinguished on the fields of Europe as the price for Wilson's romanticism. Yet today, his idealism lives on in the fanciful dreams of those who wish to recast the world in America's own image, not through institutions, but by brute force. It is the same song, merely a different verse, and we will not be taken in by this utopian vision. This great country will conduct its foreign policy on the solid ground of its considerable power and its interests, while steadfastly refusing to be intoxicated by the former. I understand that pursuing a strategy that attempts to create a stable world through deterrence and containment at this moment in history is not without its risks and may be criticized by some as too timid and cautious or, alternatively, by others as cold-hearted and immoral given the events of September 11. But regardless of how bold or pure a strategy we pursue, or how much we spend on our defenses, we cannot achieve invulnerability. We must deal with the world as it is, not as we would like it to be. And while this approach is hardly flawless, it is less risky than empire-building and less fuzzy-minded than multilateral internationalism. It steers a course consonant with our vital national interests, and it alone will secure a peaceful, safer world for successive generations of Americans.

SPEECH THREE: A COOPERATIVE WORLD ORDER

A policy that emphasizes multilateral approaches in international affairs; advocates the use of American power to strengthen norms and institutions designed to prevent the proliferation of weapons of mass destruction and to combat global poverty and growing lawlessness; adapts cooperative security arrangements to deal with the present threat environment and builds new ones; integrates former adversaries into an international system that supports our values; emphasizes preventive diplomacy; and recognizes that preemption may be necessary as a matter of last resort but counsels in favor of acting with the support of the international community.

Members of Congress and My Fellow Americans:

I have decided to speak to you this evening because we now face important decisions that will affect our national security for decades to come. The United States presently enjoys a position of unrivaled military, technological, and economic power. Yet, as we discovered on September 11, 2001, our preponderance of power does not make us invulnerable. Even as our national healing continues, we are now confronted by the danger that terrorists and the tyrants who support them are prepared to use weapons of mass destruction against us and our allies.

In this uncertain, new era, the principal challenge we face is how best to use our unprecedented power to build a safer world that is free from these terrorists and tyrants. The task before us is translating American primacy into a peace that is lasting and durable—one that, while allowing for some country-to-country variation, is roughly built around our model for national success: freedom, democracy, and free enterprise.

In the National Security Strategy that I submitted to you in September 2002, I revealed a blueprint for American foreign policy that relied on the credible threat of overwhelming military force to defeat our foes. This strategy committed us to act unilaterally, as necessary, to avoid the constraints posed by sometimes ineffectual international institutions and sluggish alliances and to do so pre-emptively in anticipation of gathering dangers. Today, I affirm that we cannot and will not wait until the moment of greatest peril is upon us. But resort to force as the centerpiece of a national strategy, either by preventive war or a dominant kind of deterrence, will not by itself be able to address the long-term causes of these threats.

A POLICY OF MULTILATERALISM

As the world's sole superpower, America has a unique set of responsibilities and burdens that requires us to use our might—sometimes alone, if necessary—to preserve peace, freedom, and prosperity. Yet, while force is occasionally a necessary evil, using it on our own has inherent limitations as a foreign policy tool. In most cases, so-called preventive war or dominant deterrence strategies are neither the ideal nor the preferred ways to transform our immense power into a global consensus in favor of our values and interests.

We cannot effectively confront the broad array of existing security threats without expanding cooperation with our allies and helping to strengthen international institutions so that they too can share security responsibilities. Moreover, only by respecting the values, judgments, and interests of our friends and partners can the United States alleviate the concerns of those countries and organizations that fear and resent our unparalleled power. Finally, global engagement and cooperation are not only strategic imperatives, but legal and moral ones as well. Achieving American foreign policy goals through consensus-building, with its implied give and take, is most consistent with how we order our domestic life and also with binding international rules of behavior.

In short, today's international climate requires that important decisions of war, peace, and development be made after consultation with other nations and international institutions. This means that the global community must play a role in defining security threats and the responses to them. As the world's preeminent power, the United States has to be the leader in forging joint action, as this is the most effective way in the long run to respond to terrorists, tyrants, and other international challenges.

In this new century, the chief purpose of American foreign policy will be to integrate other countries and institutions into arrangements consistent with U.S. interests and values. These values will be ones that not only serve America well but are also shared by the community of nations. I am referring to what I have called "the non-negotiable demands of human dignity: rule of law, limits on the power of the state, respect for women, private property, equal justice, [and] religious tolerance." We realize ours is not the only way to protect and preserve individual rights. But while the path each nation takes will necessarily vary according to its local culture and tradition, all roads should ultimately lead to freer, more open societies.

This policy will strengthen existing partnerships and build new ones in fighting international terrorism and the proliferation of weapons of mass destruction, while maintaining peace in war-torn regions. It will reach out to those who have been left behind by the economic processes of globalization and seek to turn former adversaries into stakeholders in international stability.

A multilateralist approach will allow us to take advantage of this unique moment in world history, when war between the great powers is unthinkable due to America's unprecedented military, economic, and cultural ascendancy. In a dramatic departure from the Cold War, great-power rivalry is now in abeyance. We no longer have to contain or deter imperial threats but can work in consultation and cooperation with other countries, large and small, to build a world safer for freedom, democracy, and free enterprise.

By relying on all the tools of statecraft, rather than leaning excessively on our military, this strategy is more likely to secure the peace. And by strengthening existing institutions and building new ones that enshrine liberal norms across the globe, we will extend the peace to those corners where radicalism has taken root, winning the battle for the hearts and minds of the world.

Our efforts in this regard are already delivering results. In the common struggle against al-Qaeda, we have received support from 90 nations in our military campaign in Afghanistan and from over 100 nations in our efforts to dry up the financial assets of the terrorists and arrest them before they can undertake more heinous acts. This unprecedented cooperation has led to the arrest or untimely demise of many key leaders of al-Qaeda. All told, more than 3,000 suspected terrorists have been taken into custody in a wide array of countries. And with the world's continued assistance, such extremists will continue to meet a similar fate—or worse.

THE NEED FOR A NEW INTERNATIONALISM

One thing is for certain: The United States cannot successfully wage the war on terrorism and confront other security challenges without the continued support of our allies and partners. We should be guided by the conviction that no one can build a safer world alone, no matter how vast their resources. There are a number of important reasons why we can ill afford to strike out alone.

Meeting Today's Security Challenges

Today's threats come not so much from a potential rival such as Russia or China, but from terrorists and the tyrants who harbor them. The terrorists and their state sponsors are devoting enormous energy to equip themselves with weapons of mass destruction. The problems created by the intersection of radicalism with technology will sometimes require us to use hard military power against extremists when diplomacy fails—but only as a weapon of last resort. From the 1962 Cuban missile crisis to today's situation on the Korean Peninsula, the proliferation problem has historically not been conducive to a military solution.

If we use force unsparingly, we will destroy the consensus needed to find and capture the terrorists and to cut off the supply of destructive technologies from them and their state sanctuaries. As you will hear tonight, I propose that we redouble joint law enforcement and intelligence-gathering operations against global terrorist networks, while working harder to contain outlaw regimes through arms-control initiatives and sanctions. If preventive diplomacy fails, these efforts will still have helped create a common, shared vision of the problem, which will enhance the possibilities for an American-led enforcement operation. Joint military action gives the use of force added legitimacy, making it more difficult for dictators to pursue strategies that divide allied coalitions. It also helps dispel the corrosive myth that the United States lacks concern and respect for non-Western peoples.

Consulting with our allies and partners not only confers greater legitimacy, it also conserves our own resources. As we wage war on the terrorists while simultaneously confronting rogue regimes, we must be vigilant that we do not overextend ourselves. Already, we are the world's largest debtor nation. And inside our own borders, we face a number of formidable challenges in the areas of education, health care, and preserving retirement benefits for our aging citizens. Huge increases in our military budget should not come at the price of deep cuts in vital domestic programs.

When the fighting is over, societies that have been terrorized by despotic rulers have to be rebuilt. Peacekeeping and state-building require a great deal of patience, time, and money. The experiences in Bosnia and Kosovo suggest that the real work starts when the guns fall silent. We must make sure that the United States is not forced to bear the costs of rebuilding alone. The major powers and international financial institutions have a critical role to play in ensuring that peace and stability are not short-lived. But these nations and multilateral agencies will be most willing to undertake a constructive role in this process if they are also encouraged to participate in the initial decisions about military intervention. If they are excluded from the decision-making process, we can hardly expect them to help foot the hefty bill for occupying and reconstructing nations or to continue financing our foreign debt. As several financial analysts have pointed out, when you are a net debtor to the rest of the world, you better act multilaterally.

The longer-term concern is that, should our allies feel cast aside and neglected, they may grow restless over playing host to American soldiers embarking on missions viewed as peripheral or even contrary to their national interests. Our friends may question the wisdom of welcoming U.S. troops onto their home soil for missions they themselves only half-heartedly endorse or quietly oppose. Already, such national debates are beginning to take place in a number of our European allied nations. Should this trend continue, it may jeopardize the success of future American military operations in regions vital to our national interests.

Other international challenges we face are also less amenable to a go-it-alone approach. The problem of "failed" states, such as Rwanda and Somalia in the 1990s, is now a first-order threat to our national security. When governments cannot maintain law and order in their territory, terrorists use the resulting power vacuum as a safe haven, much as al-Qaeda did in Afghanistan. We will have to work with other major powers, multilateral agencies, and nongovernmental organizations to construct domestic civil societies that respect the rule of law and yearn for democracy. A variety of other issues that have a direct impact on our nation's security— transnational crime, narcotics trafficking, global financial stability, infectious diseases, global poverty, and the environment—all require cooperation with other nations. Overwhelming military power cannot ensure success in these areas and, in some cases, might even undermine American interests, particularly if it is used unilaterally and preemptively.

Calming Fears of U.S. Hegemony

Second, working through alliances and international agreements will allay existing fears abroad that we intend to misuse our national power in service of what some perceive as illegitimate ambitions. America is a peace-loving nation. We do not seek to create empires or recast foreign societies in our own image. But in some parts of the world, the perception is mistakenly forming that we are intent on forcing others into agreement with our foreign policy agenda. Those misguided individuals who struck us on September 11 embraced this notion. As we defend our legitimate interests, we must also take care that our words and deeds show al-Qaeda's sympathizers how wrong they were about this great nation.

To some degree, resentment in other parts of the world will continue to exist by virtue of our sheer strength and the visible presence of American troops, businesses, and cultural symbols abroad. But to the extent that we are perceived as showing little regard for international rules, institutions, and cooperative frameworks that might constrain our power, we increasingly risk isolation. Some believe that we can flex our muscles and cause other major powers and multilateral organizations to fall into line with us. But history shows that great nations that use their own power arrogantly risk being encircled by countervailing coalitions.

While this may be a long-term concern, the perception overseas that the United States is unwilling to tie itself down with global rules and normative constraints already has had real and tangible consequences. For instance, the sympathy and goodwill that existed around the world after September 11 have largely dissipated, making it more difficult for us to go after terrorists and outlaw regimes. According to a recent survey of 38,000 people in 44 countries, there is widespread resentment caused by America's global influence as well as growing resistance to the perceived excesses of American leadership abroad. This message came across loud and clear this year as massive throngs of demonstrators descended on New York City and scores of other cities around the world to protest peacefully against the U.S.-led invasion of Iraq. When other countries view us as too willing to rely on our military force, rather than the rules and institutions of the international community, they are less likely to actively support our policies.

The war on terrorism is, in significant part, a struggle over the hearts and minds of the world and, in particular, the world's Islamic community. If we win the battles on the ground, but in the process lose the war over ideas, then the larger goal of producing a durable peace may be lost. We must manage to persuade others that our political, social, and economic alternatives to radicalism are not only more successful, but more compatible with the fundamental demands of human dignity.

Rather than squander our power by single-handedly deploying our forces on missions abroad, we should use it to build stronger and more durable alliances and institutions consistent with our national interests. A greater emphasis on cooperation will reassure our friends, discourage the formation of countervailing coalitions, and make sure that if and when diplomacy fails, there is a shared vision on which to launch an American-led enforcement action.

Defending the Rule of Law

Finally, not only is a multilateral approach a strategic imperative, it is a legal and moral one as well. Over half a century ago, the U.S. Senate overwhelmingly ratified the UN Charter, the principal achievement of which was to outlaw offensive wars of aggression. The charter was intended to make cataclysms such as World Wars I and II a distant memory by emphasizing collaborative, consensual processes through which competing national interests may be reconciled.

Article 51 of the UN Charter provides an exception to the prohibition on the use of force. It expressly describes an "inherent right of individual or collective self-defense" in case of an "armed attack." For several centuries, international law has recognized that nations need not literally suffer an "armed attack" first before they can take lawful action to defend themselves in the face of imminent dangers. This so-called imminence requirement for preemptive action largely originated in the United States.

In 1837, the United Kingdom worked to quell a revolt in Canada that had gained the support of private militias operating from within the United States. To discourage this foreign assistance, the British launched a night foray into New York State, burning the Americans' ship and pushing it over Niagara Falls. Several years later, Secretary of State Daniel Webster brokered a deal with the British that banned most preemptive attacks. Such raids could be legally defensible only if there was a "necessity of self-defense, instant, overwhelming, leaving no choice of means, and no moment for deliberation." Moreover, the response could not be "unreasonable or excessive." Webster's formulation has stuck with us today as part of the core of international law.

So, in principle, America has legal grounds to act alone, if necessary, to exercise the right of self-defense. But international law also suggests that we be cautious in how broadly we define this right. Our tradition of fighting "just wars" requires us to consider such issues as whether the preemptive action is taken as a last resort, whether there is a reasonable chance of success, and whether the action is proportional to the threat. When it is possible, we will present compelling evidence to the UN Security Council that terrorist groups or outlaw regimes linked to them are nearing a capability to launch an imminent strike against the American homeland, troops, interests, or allies. In each case, this capability should also be matched by an intent to lash out against American interests. As I will explain, our policy toward Iraq is being conducted precisely in this manner.

September 11 has shown that we are up against a terrorist enemy who is willing and able to unleash wanton destruction and inflict untold casualties on America. The terrorists seek martyrdom and operate without addresses, making traditional concepts of deterrence problematic. We also have evidence that they are presently pursuing weapons of mass destruction and will not hesitate to use them against us. Under these circumstances, I believe that international law permits us to take preemptive action against al-Qaeda and its terrorist siblings.

Similarly, the overlap between states that sponsor terror and those that pursue weapons of mass destruction may compel us to action. But before we use force, we will consult with the UN Security Council and our allies, asking for their approval after presenting clear evidence of the gathering danger. While neither the UN nor our friends exercise a veto power over our own security, the United States will work with them to explain why we think that, in their present incarnations, deterrence and containment vis-à-vis outlaw regimes have achieved only modest results. We have thus far adhered to this consultative formula in our Iraq policy, beginning with my speech to the UN on September 12, 2002. That led to the passage of Security Council Resolution 1441 in November 2002, which formed the legal basis for the coalition that invaded Iraq on March 17, 2003.

If the United States acts hastily, without building international support, our enforcement actions will lose their legitimacy, with the potentially serious consequences I outlined above. Past U.S. presidents have understood this idea well. For instance, even during the Cuban missile crisis—arguably the gravest threat that our country has ever faced—President Kennedy refused to launch a preemptive strike on Cuba in the name of "anticipatory self-defense." He opted against the recommendations of his military advisers, instead relying on the regional peacekeeping provisions of the UN Charter to interdict Soviet ships on the high seas.

Furthermore, if we are perceived as invoking an expansive, fact-free concept of preemptive self-defense, we may unwittingly invite other nations to use similar claims as a smoke screen for launching military campaigns to pursue their own national interests. Russia could try to make its own case for preemptive action against Georgia on the grounds that that country has not acted swiftly to get rid of terrorists operating within its borders. Similarly, India may seek to justify preemptive action against Pakistan by linking that state to ongoing terrorism in Kashmir, while Israel could make a similar line of argument to justify preemption of the Palestinian Authority. In short, precipitous unilateral action by the world's only superpower risks creating a precedent that leads to a more dangerous, uncertain world for us as well as our allies and partners.

THE RESPONSE TO NEW CHALLENGES

The best way for America to reconcile its unparalleled power with its vulnerability to so-called asymmetric security threats is to integrate other nations and institutions into arrangements consistent with our interests and values. Tonight I am proposing a four-pronged plan of action designed to reinvigorate the global nonproliferation regime; work with our allies and partners to deter and contain rogue states; strengthen relationships with traditional allies and toil together to redefine existing security organizations; and, finally, integrate former adversaries into international institutions.

Reinvigorating the Nonproliferation Regime
Now that the Cold War has ended, we no longer live in fear of a nuclear winter. But more than a decade after the Berlin Wall fell, the civilized world faces a new threat from terrorists and irresponsible leaders who might work alone or collude to acquire weapons of mass destruction (whether nuclear, biological, or chemical) and use them against the United States. The first line of defense against radicalism is the interlocking set of treaties and institutions that form the global nonproliferation regime. I will work to strengthen traditional measures—diplomacy, arms-control treaties, cooperative threat-reduction initiatives, and export controls—that seek to check state proliferators and terrorist networks.

In particular, the United States will place a premium on helping secure the fissile materials and nuclear weapons of the former Soviet Union, since this may be the most likely place for terrorists to get their hands on weapons of mass destruction. I pledge to expand significantly the budget of the Nunn-Lugar program and other initiatives designed to help Russia deal safely with its Cold War legacy of nuclear, biological, and chemical weapons–related expertise and materials.

At the same time, we will solidify the norms against proliferation through multilateral regimes. The United States will strengthen the nuclear Nonproliferation Treaty and the International Atomic Energy Agency by ratifying an IAEA Additional Protocol, asking for assurances that all states implement full-scope IAEA safeguards agreements, and proposing increases in that agency's funding. We will negotiate a fissile material cutoff treaty and participate in steps to strengthen the Nuclear Suppliers Group and the Zangger Committee. The United States will also propose measures for the more effective implementation of the Chemical Weapons Convention, including an improved inspection system. In addition, we will resume our participation in the meetings called to develop a biological weapons protocol and identify constructive ways to verify and enforce obligations under the Biological Weapons Convention—a binding treaty actually proposed by President Nixon 30 years ago. Finally, I will spend whatever political capital is needed to secure the two-thirds vote necessary for

Senate ratification of the Comprehensive Test Ban Treaty, whose intrusive verification regime will reduce incentives for states to proliferate. As a report from a former chairman of the Joint Chiefs of Staff noted, stemming the proliferation of destructive technologies can be accomplished without jeopardizing the safety and reliability of our own nuclear arsenal.

Other foreign policy tools such as national export controls and nonproliferation sanctions will play an important role in this agenda as well. While being sure not to unnecessarily undermine American commercial interests, we will revise and strengthen existing export-control authorities, with a focus on regulating truly sensitive exports to hostile regimes. The United States will also develop a comprehensive sanctions policy that is more flexible and responsive to the causes of proliferation, while reducing the unintended, collateral impact on foreign civilians.

At the same time, the U.S. military will be prepared to deter and defend against the full range of contingencies outlined in the Pentagon's 2001 Quadrennial Defense Review. We will adapt interdiction and deterrence to confront today's threats effectively, as I will discuss in detail later. As part of our National Security Strategy, preempting an imminent attack will remain an option, but anticipatory self-defense will not be the centerpiece of our efforts to combat the proliferation of weapons of mass destruction. Preemption is a single quiver in our foreign policy arsenal; it will not be elevated to the level of dogma or grand strategy.

Deterring and Containing Rogue Regimes

One of the most serious security problems we face is how to handle dictators intent on acquiring weapons of mass destruction. The heads of these outlaw regimes covet catastrophic weapons to use to blackmail the United States, bully their neighbors, and extract concessions from the rest of the world. We will redouble our efforts to deter and contain rogue regimes. In each instance, the United States will tailor its specific policies to the circumstances of the country at issue, rather than adopt a one-size-fits-all approach. As part of our strategy, we will seek to impress on our partners and allies the grave nature of these threats. But while we strive to achieve consensus, we will not surrender decision-making to international organizations that fail to achieve results.

The main goal of U.S. foreign policy toward Iraq was to separate Saddam Hussein from his weapons of mass destruction. Our preferred method of accomplishing this task was through vigorous diplomatic efforts designed to rebuild the multilateral coalition that once stood strong against this most dangerous Arab nation. More than ten years ago, the international community followed American leadership to tie down Saddam's power-mad regime in what was the most formidable global fighting force ever assembled. In the intervening decade, Iraq systematically flouted the will of the community of nations, embodied in UN Security Council resolutions, leaving us no choice but to lead a coalition of the willing to remove Saddam from power.

Iraq's neighbor Iran is presently caught in a tug-of-war between a pro-reform, democratically elected government and a pervasively anti-American clergy that wields significant political power. In the future, the mullahs' harsh conservatism will be their undoing. Time is on our side. But until that moment arrives, we will work with Iran's neighbors—particularly Russia—and the United Nations to make sure that country's quest for nuclear weapons ends in failure. In building a global consensus against Iran's active nuclear programs, we will make every effort to convince Moscow to side with us in denying Tehran access to technologies that will fulfill its nuclear ambitions.

Tensions have also been on the rise on the Korean Peninsula. North Korea has been violating international law—and solemn agreements made with the United States and its allies—by secretly obtaining the means to produce weapons-grade uranium. Now there is word that this nation is feverishly working to process plutonium for a sizeable atomic arsenal. The North must know that we stand determined and ready in the face of its nuclear blackmail. Yet the path to peace and stability on the peninsula does not presently call for the preemptive use of force. Rather, the United States will work closely with our allies and partners—most prominently South Korea, Japan, Russia, and China—to negotiate a broad, stringent, and verifiable agreement that closes North Korea's nuclear weapons and missile facilities and its related export business for good. As President Kennedy noted some 40 years ago, we shall never negotiate out of fear, but we must also never fear to negotiate. Pyongyang will soon learn that it cannot expect to gain political recognition and economic aid unless it abjures its ruinous pursuit of nuclear weapons.

Building Effective Cooperative Security Arrangements
At present, U.S. troops, ships, and aircraft stationed in the Persian Gulf and on the Korean Peninsula are helping to enforce international norms. And we will not shrink from the unique responsibilities that come with our military and economic strength. But in the future, the United States cannot and should not have to deal with lawbreakers and "failed" states largely on its own. Let's be honest. At present, the international community lacks the ability to buttress its diplomacy with an international military force. In the last decade, our global institutions and alliances have struggled to manage conflicts that have erupted in places such as Afghanistan, Bosnia, Haiti, Iraq, Kosovo, Rwanda, and Somalia.

In the coming years, the United States will rely on preventive diplomacy and humanitarian assistance to resolve problems before they explode into wars. But when these efforts fail, we need something more effective to restore international peace and security. Other than doing the job alone, the two choices we have before us are to rely on the United Nations or to rely on our regional allies.

Our initial efforts to hand over enforcement responsibilities to the United Nations shortly after its creation in 1945 were well intentioned but premature. Then, once the Cold War set in, the possibilities for collective military action were frustrated. But at this unique moment in history, while our power is unrivaled and most other major nations share a common vision of the threats to international security, we must move forward with the unfinished project of creating a permanent standing force. I will ask the UN Security Council and the secretary-general to place this issue at the top of their agenda. This force will not develop overnight, and its realization will require overcoming significant obstacles. In the interim, we will suggest that the UN Security Council immediately consider how to gain more reliable access to well-trained and well-equipped forces for peacekeeping and peace-enforcement missions.

The UN is not the only institution that preserves global stability. America is blessed with many friends who share our love for freedom and democracy. Our allies in Europe and Asia also share common interests in fighting terrorists with global reach, stemming the spread of weapons of mass destruction, and preventing anarchy from descending on "failed" states. Our experiences in Afghanistan, Bosnia, the 1991 Persian Gulf War with Iraq, and Kosovo suggest that, when the United States assumes a leadership role in defense of these common interests, collective military action can work.

Our challenge is to find a new role for existing collective-security arrangements and create new ones responsive to 21st-century problems. In Europe, we must work harder with our long-standing friends and allies now that the threat from communism has receded. At the top of our transatlantic agenda is forging a common vision for NATO that keeps it central to U.S. foreign policy priorities, not only as a political organization, but also as a military alliance.

For our part, the United States will take care to heed the concerns of NATO members in setting the new agenda, even as we seek to enlist their cooperation outside Europe's borders, particularly in the greater Middle East. We will seek to expand NATO's membership to include democratic nations willing and able to advance our common interests. At the same time, European nations will have to devote greater resources to their defenses in order to ensure they can make an appropriate contribution to multinational fighting forces and participate in the technological revolution in military affairs. We will encourage other NATO countries to lead smaller security missions where their interests are greater than ours. To this end, I am pleased to hear of the European Union's commitment to building a force of 60,000 rapid-reaction troops in the near future to respond to crises. And I hope our friends in Europe promptly back up their words with the resources, technology, and personnel to make this plan a reality.

In Asia, we will similarly work with our allies, including Japan, South Korea, the Philippines, Thailand, and Australia, to build a security architecture consistent with our shared interests. Our friends in Asia realize that the terrorists have their sights trained on them as well. The recent cowardly attacks in Bali are just one reminder that the struggle against terror has been and will continue to be a global one. We intend to use our long-standing relationships with our treaty allies to build a strong foundation for new types of multilateral cooperation against global terror networks and other threats to stability.

Finally, national security in this era of globalization requires us to do more than merely institutionalize cooperation against traditional threats. We must take the reins in multilateral organizations to build mutually beneficial trade relationships, increase foreign direct investment in the developing world, alleviate global poverty, and fight infectious diseases. For instance, a report released recently by the National Intelligence Council warned that the HIV/AIDS pandemic continues to spread around the world at an alarming rate. It estimates that AIDS cases, which now number 65 million, will triple by 2010. I have asked Congress to be a leader in the world's struggle against this scourge by pledging $15 billion over the next five years for the Emergency Plan for AIDS Relief in Africa and the Caribbean.

But we can and must do more. The World Health Organization has asked this country to contribute $10 billion a year, the annual cost of developing the national missile defense system, to fight infectious diseases in poor countries. The organization argues correctly that this program could save millions of lives each year. The amount of development and food aid that the United States has budgeted for all of Africa is a paltry $1.1 billion. By comparison, the price of a single B-2 bomber is nearly double that figure. Violence, discrimination, and disenfranchisement must not be seen as problems for the poor and the weak to face alone. We need only look to Afghanistan to see what can happen if our government turns a blind eye to the humiliation and suffering endured by others. Just as we are leading the world in the fight against terrorism with a global reach, we need to lead a global campaign against poverty, hunger and disease.

Integrating Former Adversaries into International Institutions
While we renew cooperation with historical allies, we must also set aside the memories of past antagonisms with former adversaries. Several major powers are in the process of significant political or economic transition, or both; most prominent among these are Russia, China, and India. We remain aware of the possibility of a return to great-power competition but are encouraged by recent developments that suggest our values and goals are increasingly being shared by these nations. Even where differences exist, American interests are best served by an approach that seeks to integrate Russia, China, and India into institutions that will help build a safer, more prosperous world.

We have already begun to forge a new strategic partnership with Russia. Our common response to the tragedy of September 11 has brought our two nations closer together in ways that once did not appear possible. The United States will take advantage of the shift in Russian thinking by broadening our cooperation in several areas. We will strengthen our coordinated efforts in the war on terrorism and assist Russia as it prepares itself for entry into the World Trade Organization. Along with our transatlantic allies, we have established the NATO-Russia Council to deepen Russia's cooperation on security issues with Europe and ourselves. But while our relations have improved, we harbor no illusions as to Russia's uneven commitment to free-market, democratic values and global nonproliferation norms. We will continue to raise these issues with Russia, as part of a broader framework that seeks to integrate that country into the Euro-Atlantic community.

Our relationship with China is an important part of our strategy to maintain a peaceful, stable, and secure Asia-Pacific region. We are encouraged by China's cooperation in the war on terrorism, its assistance in dealing with North Korea's nuclear situation, and its recent entry into the World Trade Organization. Yet we cannot ignore our differences—in particular, on issues of human rights, proliferation of weapons of mass destruction, and

Taiwan. The United States is working to narrow our areas of disagreement, while not allowing them to impede cooperation on matters of common concern. As China's power grows, the best way to ensure it remains a benign, status quo country is to enmesh it in a web of regional and multilateral institutions that strengthens its respect for the rule of law.

Finally, the U.S. relationship with India has entered a new era. As the world's two largest democracies, both characterized by diverse, multiethnic societies, India and America have much in common. From its birth, India, like America, has had a commitment to representative institutions that protect political and religious freedom. Now it has also begun to accelerate its transition to free-market economic principles. While differences linger, including over India's nuclear and missile programs, these concerns will no longer impede stronger diplomatic and commercial ties that lie in the interests of both nations.

At a time when the major powers are united by common security threats, we must work together to build what I have called "a balance of power that favors freedom." The events of September 11 fundamentally changed the global security landscape, creating vast new opportunities for cooperation, not only with our allies in Europe and Asia, but with Russia, China, and India as well. We are committed to seizing this chance to create durable, lasting ties that create a world safer for free-market democracy.

A FORCE MULTIPLIER IN FAVOR OF FREEDOM

Our unrivaled military and economic power in this "unipolar moment" provides a unique window of opportunity in which to try to build a safer, more peaceful world modeled on universal, democratic values. There are some who advise that the best way to accomplish this goal is to use our forces, alone, if necessary, to defend and extend the peace. They contend that although our means might be unilateral, the ends we serve are global. The rest of the world will eventually appreciate our bold and decisive response to today's perils, the argument goes.

But I believe we cannot simply recast outlaw states in our own image by threatening and using military force. This strategy breeds resentment, fosters countervailing coalitions, and over-burdens our resources. Over the long haul, it might also weaken the fabric of domestic institutions vital to our own democracy by unduly strengthening the executive and replacing norms of accountability and transparency with secrecy. Ultimately, I fear this approach will collapse under the weight of its overweening ambition, and we will have lost an opportunity to mold the world into a safer, more secure place. Rather than rule by decree, the only way to achieve security is to build a global consensus that supports American values.

Let no one mistake my message. America's military is strong—and we intend to keep it that way. Our troops are the linchpin of stability in every region of the world, from Asia to Europe, from Latin America to the Middle East. We are constantly working to re-equip, retrain, and reorganize our forces to respond to the new security threats we face today. But I am mindful of the temptation to rely too much on our armed forces, at the expense of our other foreign policy tools. We cannot have a one-dimensional foreign policy. We need to rely on smart diplomats as well as smart weapons. Military dominance should not be our mantra, an end to be pursued in itself. Paradoxically, as the Pentagon's own war games have demonstrated, such pursuit of military dominance could make us less secure in the long run because it may give our adversaries or potential adversaries, who have no hope of competing with our conventional military power, an incentive to develop nuclear weapons. If we fall victim to this trap, we will let slip away this moment of unparalleled strength and potentially be left with a world full of determined enemies and reluctant allies. Far from representing weak-minded altruism, this policy operates on the firm ground of our own enlightened self-interest.

In the future, all our power resources will be increasingly used to strengthen the international system that we took the leadership in creating after World War II. Every significant global institution—the UN, NATO, the World Bank, the International Monetary Fund, and the global trading regime—was made in America.

They lie at the forefront of the rising tide of democracies and free markets that is sweeping the globe. We will use our considerable voice in these institutions to create peace and stability by identifying and consolidating the common ground for cooperation, co-opting "failed" states, isolating outlaw regimes, and, most important, defeating terrorists.

I understand that this strategy is not without its own risks. At times, other countries will have interests that conflict with our own, and so they will seek to frustrate our legitimate aims through protracted negotiations. We cannot always afford to wait for consensus to emerge as dangers gather over the horizon. That is why, when collective action proves unmanageable, the United States will reserve the option to strike out alone or with a coalition of the willing, as we did against Iraq in the spring of 2003. But when we do so, it will preferably be not only in our own defense, but in support of widely held norms that have been systematically transgressed. We will endeavor to take such action selectively and after consultation with our allies, so as not to fatally weaken institutions that generally serve our own interests.

Henry Kissinger said it best: The "test of history for the United States will be whether we can turn our current predominant power into international consensus and our own principles into widely accepted international norms." A strategy of working through strengthened alliances and institutions is the one most likely to secure the blessings of peace and freedom. It tempers our immense strength with a far-sighted patience and humility, winning over friends while isolating enemies. Today's methods will necessarily be different from past ones, but the outcome will remain the same: a safer future for America and, through cooperation in the common interest, for the rest of the world as well.

APPENDIXES

APPENDIX A: THE NATIONAL SECURITY STRATEGY OF THE UNITED STATES OF AMERICA, SEPTEMBER 2002

The great struggles of the twentieth century between liberty and totalitarianism ended with a decisive victory for the forces of freedom—and a single sustainable model for national success: freedom, democracy, and free enterprise. In the twenty-first century, only nations that share a commitment to protecting basic human rights and guaranteeing political and economic freedom will be able to unleash the potential of their people and assure their future prosperity. People everywhere want to be able to speak freely; choose who will govern them; worship as they please; educate their children—male and female; own property; and enjoy the benefits of their labor. These values of freedom are right and true for every person, in every society—and the duty of protecting these values against their enemies is the common calling of freedom-loving people across the globe and across the ages.

Today, the United States enjoys a position of unparalleled military strength and great economic and political influence. In keeping with our heritage and principles, we do not use our strength to press for unilateral advantage. We seek instead to create a balance of power that favors human freedom: conditions in which all nations and all societies can choose for themselves the rewards and challenges of political and economic liberty. In a world that is safe, people will be able to make their own lives better. We will defend the peace by fighting terrorists and tyrants. We will preserve the peace by building good relations among the great powers. We will extend the peace by encouraging free and open societies on every continent.

Defending our Nation against its enemies is the first and fundamental commitment of the Federal Government. Today, that task has changed dramatically. Enemies in the past needed great armies and great industrial capabilities to endanger America.

Now, shadowy networks of individuals can bring great chaos and suffering to our shores for less than it costs to purchase a single tank. Terrorists are organized to penetrate open societies and to turn the power of modern technologies against us.

To defeat this threat we must make use of every tool in our arsenal—military power, better homeland defenses, law enforcement, intelligence, and vigorous efforts to cut off terrorist financing. The war against terrorists of global reach is a global enterprise of uncertain duration. America will help nations that need our assistance in combating terror. And America will hold to account nations that are compromised by terror, including those who harbor terrorists—because the allies of terror are the enemies of civilization. The United States and countries cooperating with us must not allow the terrorists to develop new home bases. Together, we will seek to deny them sanctuary at every turn.

The gravest danger our Nation faces lies at the crossroads of radicalism and technology. Our enemies have openly declared that they are seeking weapons of mass destruction, and evidence indicates that they are doing so with determination. The United States will not allow these efforts to succeed. We will build defenses against ballistic missiles and other means of delivery. We will cooperate with other nations to deny, contain, and curtail our enemies' efforts to acquire dangerous technologies. And, as a matter of common sense and self-defense, America will act against such emerging threats before they are fully formed. We cannot defend America and our friends by hoping for the best. So we must be prepared to defeat our enemies' plans, using the best intelligence and proceeding with deliberation. History will judge harshly those who saw this coming danger but failed to act. In the new world we have entered, the only path to peace and security is the path of action.

As we defend the peace, we will also take advantage of an historic opportunity to preserve the peace. Today, the international community has the best chance since the rise of the nation-state in the seventeenth century to build a world where great powers compete in peace instead of continually prepare for war. Today, the world's great powers find ourselves on the same side—united by common dangers of terrorist violence and chaos. The United States will build on these common interests to promote global security. We are also increasingly united by common values. Russia is in the midst of a hopeful transition, reaching for its democratic future and a partner in the war on terror. Chinese leaders are discovering that economic freedom is the only source of national wealth. In time, they will find that social and political freedom is the only source of national greatness. America will encourage the advancement of democracy and economic openness in both nations, because these are the best foundations for domestic stability and international order. We will strongly resist aggression from other great powers—even as we welcome their peaceful pursuit of prosperity, trade, and cultural advancement.

Finally, the United States will use this moment of opportunity to extend the benefits of freedom across the globe. We will actively work to bring the hope of democracy, development, free markets, and free trade to every corner of the world. The events of September 11, 2001, taught us that weak states, like Afghanistan, can pose as great a danger to our national interests as strong states. Poverty does not make poor people into terrorists and murderers. Yet poverty, weak institutions, and corruption can make weak states vulnerable to terrorist networks and drug cartels within their borders.

The United States will stand beside any nation determined to build a better future by seeking the rewards of liberty for its people. Free trade and free markets have proven their ability to lift whole societies out of poverty—so the United States will work with individual nations, entire regions, and the entire global trading community to build a world that trades in freedom and therefore grows in prosperity. The United States will deliver greater development assistance through the New Millennium Challenge Account to nations that govern justly, invest in their people, and encourage economic freedom. We will also continue to lead the world in efforts to reduce the terrible toll of HIV/AIDS and other infectious diseases.

In building a balance of power that favors freedom, the United States is guided by the conviction that all nations have important responsibilities. Nations that enjoy freedom must actively fight terror. Nations that depend on international stability must help prevent the spread of weapons of mass destruction. Nations that seek international aid must govern themselves wisely, so that aid is well spent. For freedom to thrive, accountability must be expected and required.

We are also guided by the conviction that no nation can build a safer, better world alone. Alliances and multilateral institutions can multiply the strength of freedom-loving nations. The United States is committed to lasting institutions like the United Nations, the World Trade Organization, the Organization of American States, and NATO as well as other long-standing alliances. Coalitions of the willing can augment these permanent institutions. In all cases, international obligations are to be taken seriously. They are not to be undertaken symbolically to rally support for an ideal without furthering its attainment.

Freedom is the non-negotiable demand of human dignity; the birthright of every person—in every civilization. Throughout history, freedom has been threatened by war and terror; it has been challenged by the clashing wills of powerful states and the evil designs of tyrants; and it has been tested by widespread poverty and disease. Today, humanity holds in its hands the opportunity to further freedom's triumph over all these foes. The United States welcomes our responsibility to lead in this great mission.

George W. Bush
The White House
September 17, 2002

Appendix A: The National Security Strategy

I. OVERVIEW OF AMERICA'S INTERNATIONAL STRATEGY

"Our Nation's cause has always been larger than our Nation's defense. We fight, as we always fight, for a just peace—a peace that favors liberty. We will defend the peace against the threats from terrorists and tyrants. We will preserve the peace by building good relations among the great powers. And we will extend the peace by encouraging free and open societies on every continent."

President Bush
West Point, New York
June 1, 2002

The United States possesses unprecedented—and unequaled—strength and influence in the world. Sustained by faith in the principles of liberty, and the value of a free society, this position comes with unparalleled responsibilities, obligations, and opportunity. The great strength of this nation must be used to promote a balance of power that favors freedom.

For most of the twentieth century, the world was divided by a great struggle over ideas: destructive totalitarian visions versus freedom and equality.

That great struggle is over. The militant visions of class, nation, and race which promised utopia and delivered misery have been defeated and discredited. America is now threatened less by conquering states than we are by failing ones. We are menaced less by fleets and armies than by catastrophic technologies in the hands of the embittered few. We must defeat these threats to our Nation, allies, and friends.

This is also a time of opportunity for America. We will work to translate this moment of influence into decades of peace, prosperity, and liberty. The U.S. national security strategy will be based on a distinctly American internationalism that reflects the union of our values and our national interests. The aim of this strategy is to help make the world not just safer but better. Our goals on the path to progress are clear: political and economic freedom, peaceful relations with other states, and respect for human dignity.

And this path is not America's alone. It is open to all. To achieve these goals, the United States will:

- champion aspirations for human dignity;

- strengthen alliances to defeat global terrorism and work to prevent attacks against us and our friends;

- work with others to defuse regional conflicts;

- prevent our enemies from threatening us, our allies, and our friends, with weapons of mass destruction;

- ignite a new era of global economic growth through free markets and free trade;

- expand the circle of development by opening societies and building the infrastructure of democracy;

- develop agendas for cooperative action with other main centers of global power; and

- transform America's national security institutions to meet the challenges and opportunities of the twenty-first century.

II. CHAMPION ASPIRATIONS FOR HUMAN DIGNITY

"Some worry that it is somehow undiplomatic or impolite to speak the language of right and wrong. I disagree. Different circumstances require different methods, but not different moralities."

President Bush
West Point, New York
June 1, 2002

In pursuit of our goals, our first imperative is to clarify what we stand for: the United States must defend liberty and justice because these principles are right and true for all people everywhere.

No nation owns these aspirations, and no nation is exempt from them. Fathers and mothers in all societies want their children to be educated and to live free from poverty and violence. No people on earth yearn to be oppressed, aspire to servitude, or eagerly await the midnight knock of the secret police.

America must stand firmly for the nonnegotiable demands of human dignity: the rule of law; limits on the absolute power of the state; free speech; freedom of worship; equal justice; respect for women; religious and ethnic tolerance; and respect for private property.

These demands can be met in many ways. America's constitution has served us well. Many other nations, with different histories and cultures, facing different circumstances, have successfully incorporated these core principles into their own systems of governance. History has not been kind to those nations which ignored or flouted the rights and aspirations of their people.

America's experience as a great multi-ethnic democracy affirms our conviction that people of many heritages and faiths can live and prosper in peace. Our own history is a long struggle to live up to our ideals. But even in our worst moments, the principles enshrined in the Declaration of Independence were there to guide us. As a result, America is not just a stronger, but is a freer and more just society.

Today, these ideals are a lifeline to lonely defenders of liberty. And when openings arrive, we can encourage change—as we did in central and eastern Europe between 1989 and 1991, or in Belgrade in 2000. When we see democratic processes take hold among our friends in Taiwan or in the Republic of Korea, and see elected leaders replace generals in Latin America and Africa, we see examples of how authoritarian systems can evolve, marrying local history and traditions with the principles we all cherish.

Embodying lessons from our past and using the opportunity we have today, the national security strategy of the United States must start from these core beliefs and look outward for possibilities to expand liberty.

Our principles will guide our government's decisions about international cooperation, the character of our foreign assistance, and the allocation of resources. They will guide our actions and our words in international bodies.

We will:

- speak out honestly about violations of the nonnegotiable demands of human dignity using our voice and vote in international institutions to advance freedom;

- use our foreign aid to promote freedom and support those who struggle non-violently for it, ensuring that nations moving toward democracy are rewarded for the steps they take;

- make freedom and the development of democratic institutions key themes in our bilateral relations, seeking solidarity and cooperation from other democracies while we press governments that deny human rights to move toward a better future; and

- take special efforts to promote freedom of religion and conscience and defend it from encroachment by repressive governments.

We will champion the cause of human dignity and oppose those who resist it.

III. STRENGTHEN ALLIANCES TO DEFEAT GLOBAL
TERRORISM AND WORK TO PREVENT ATTACKS AGAINST US
AND OUR FRIENDS

"Just three days removed from these events, Americans do not yet have the distance of history. But our responsibility to history is already clear: to answer these attacks and rid the world of evil. War has been waged against us by stealth and deceit and murder. This nation is peaceful, but fierce when stirred to anger. The conflict was begun on the timing and terms of others. It will end in a way, and at an hour, of our choosing."

President Bush
Washington, D.C. (The National Cathedral)
September 14, 2001

The United States of America is fighting a war against terrorists of global reach. The enemy is not a single political regime or person or religion or ideology. The enemy is terrorism—premeditated, politically motivated violence perpetrated against innocents.

In many regions, legitimate grievances prevent the emergence of a lasting peace. Such grievances deserve to be, and must be, addressed within a political process. But no cause justifies terror. The United States will make no concessions to terrorist demands and strike no deals with them. We make no distinction between terrorists and those who knowingly harbor or provide aid to them.

The struggle against global terrorism is different from any other war in our history. It will be fought on many fronts against a particularly elusive enemy over an extended period of time. Progress will come through the persistent accumulation of successes—some seen, some unseen.

Today our enemies have seen the results of what civilized nations can, and will, do against regimes that harbor, support, and use terrorism to achieve their political goals. Afghanistan has been liberated; coalition forces continue to hunt down the Taliban and al-Qaida. But it is not only this battlefield on which we will engage terrorists. Thousands of trained terrorists remain at large with cells in North America, South America, Europe, Africa, the Middle East, and across Asia.

Our priority will be first to disrupt and destroy terrorist organizations of global reach and attack their leadership; command, control, and communications; material support; and finances. This will have a disabling effect upon the terrorists' ability to plan and operate.

We will continue to encourage our regional partners to take up a coordinated effort that isolates the terrorists. Once the regional campaign localizes the threat to a particular state, we will help ensure the state has the military, law enforcement, political, and financial tools necessary to finish the task.

The United States will continue to work with our allies to disrupt the financing of terrorism. We will identify and block the sources of funding for terrorism, freeze the assets of terrorists and those who support them, deny terrorists access to the international financial system, protect legitimate charities from being abused by terrorists, and prevent the movement of terrorists' assets through alternative financial networks.

However, this campaign need not be sequential to be effective; the cumulative effect across all regions will help achieve the results we seek. We will disrupt and destroy terrorist organizations by:

- direct and continuous action using all the elements of national and international power. Our immediate focus will be those terrorist organizations of global reach and any terrorist or state sponsor of terrorism which attempts to gain or use weapons of mass destruction (WMD) or their precursors;

- defending the United States, the American people, and our interests at home and abroad by identifying and destroying the threat before it reaches our borders. While the United States will constantly strive to enlist the support of the international community, we will not hesitate to act alone, if necessary, to exercise our right of self-defense by acting preemptively against such terrorists, to prevent them from doing harm against our people and our country; and

- denying further sponsorship, support, and sanctuary to terrorists by convincing or compelling states to accept their sovereign responsibilities. We will also wage a war of ideas to win the battle against international terrorism. This includes:

  - using the full influence of the United States, and working closely with allies and friends, to make clear that all acts of terrorism are illegitimate so that terrorism will be viewed in the same light as slavery, piracy, or genocide: behavior that no respectable government can condone or support and all must oppose;

  - supporting moderate and modern government, especially in the Muslim world, to ensure that the conditions and ideologies that promote terrorism do not find fertile ground in any nation;

- diminishing the underlying conditions that spawn terrorism by enlisting the international community to focus its efforts and resources on areas most at risk; and

- using effective public diplomacy to promote the free flow of information and ideas to kindle the hopes and aspirations of freedom of those in societies ruled by the sponsors of global terrorism.

While we recognize that our best defense is a good offense, we are also strengthening America's homeland security to protect against and deter attack. This Administration has proposed the largest government reorganization since the Truman Administration created the National Security Council and the Department of Defense. Centered on a new Department of Homeland Security and including a new unified military command and a fundamental reordering of the FBI, our comprehensive plan to secure the homeland encompasses every level of government and the cooperation of the public and the private sector.

This strategy will turn adversity into opportunity. For example, emergency management systems will be better able to cope not just with terrorism but with all hazards. Our medical system will be strengthened to manage not just bioterror, but all infectious diseases and mass-casualty dangers. Our border controls will not just stop terrorists, but improve the efficient movement of legitimate traffic.

While our focus is protecting America, we know that to defeat terrorism in today's globalized world we need support from our allies and friends. Wherever possible, the United States will rely on regional organizations and state powers to meet their obligations to fight terrorism. Where governments find the fight against terrorism beyond their capacities, we will match their willpower and their resources with whatever help we and our allies can provide.

As we pursue the terrorists in Afghanistan, we will continue to work with international organizations such as the United Nations, as well as non-governmental organizations, and other countries to provide the humanitarian, political, economic, and security assistance necessary to rebuild Afghanistan so that it will never again abuse its people, threaten its neighbors, and provide a haven for terrorists.

In the war against global terrorism, we will never forget that we are ultimately fighting for our democratic values and way of life. Freedom and fear are at war, and there will be no quick or easy end to this conflict. In leading the campaign against terrorism, we are forging new, productive international relationships and redefining existing ones in ways that meet the challenges of the twenty-first century.

IV. WORK WITH OTHERS TO DEFUSE REGIONAL CONFLICTS

"We build a world of justice, or we will live in a world of coercion. The magnitude of our shared responsibilities makes our disagreements look so small."

President Bush
Berlin, Germany
May 23, 2002

Concerned nations must remain actively engaged in critical regional disputes to avoid explosive escalation and minimize human suffering. In an increasingly interconnected world, regional crisis can strain our alliances, rekindle rivalries among the major powers, and create horrifying affronts to human dignity. When violence erupts and states falter, the United States will work with friends and partners to alleviate suffering and restore stability.

No doctrine can anticipate every circumstance in which U.S. action—direct or indirect—is warranted. We have finite political, economic, and military resources to meet our global priorities. The United States will approach each case with these strategic principles in mind:

- The United States should invest time and resources into building international relationships and institutions that can help manage local crises when they emerge.

- The United States should be realistic about its ability to help those who are unwilling or unready to help themselves. Where and when people are ready to do their part, we will be willing to move decisively.

The Israeli-Palestinian conflict is critical because of the toll of human suffering, because of America's close relationship with the state of Israel and key Arab states, and because of that region's importance to other global priorities of the United States. There can be no peace for either side without freedom for both sides. America stands committed to an independent and democratic Palestine, living beside Israel in peace and security. Like all other people, Palestinians deserve a government that serves their interests and listens to their voices. The United States will continue to encourage all parties to step up to their responsibilities as we seek a just and comprehensive settlement to the conflict.

The United States, the international donor community, and the World Bank stand ready to work with a reformed Palestinian government on economic development, increased humanitarian assistance, and a program to establish, finance, and monitor a truly independent judiciary. If Palestinians embrace democracy, and the rule of law, confront corruption, and firmly reject terror, they can count on American support for the creation of a Palestinian state.

Israel also has a large stake in the success of a democratic Palestine. Permanent occupation threatens Israel's identity and democracy. So the United States continues to challenge Israeli leaders to take concrete steps to support the emergence of a viable, credible Palestinian state. As there is progress towards security, Israel[i] forces need to withdraw fully to positions they held prior to September 28, 2000. And consistent with the recommendations of the Mitchell Committee, Israeli settlement activity in the occupied territories must stop. As violence subsides, freedom of movement should be restored, permitting innocent Palestinians to resume work and normal life. The United States can play a crucial role but, ultimately, lasting peace can only come when Israelis and Palestinians resolve the issues and end the conflict between them.

In South Asia, the United States has also emphasized the need for India and Pakistan to resolve their disputes. This Administration invested time and resources building strong bilateral relations with India and Pakistan. These strong relations then gave us leverage to play a constructive role when tensions in the region became acute. With Pakistan, our bilateral relations have been bolstered by Pakistan's choice to join the war against terror and move toward building a more open and tolerant society. The Administration sees India's potential to become one of the great democratic powers of the twenty-first century and has worked hard to transform our relationship accordingly. Our involvement in this regional dispute, building on earlier investments in bilateral relations, looks first to concrete steps by India and Pakistan that can help defuse military confrontation.

Indonesia took courageous steps to create a working democracy and respect for the rule of law. By tolerating ethnic minorities, respecting the rule of law, and accepting open markets, Indonesia may be able to employ the engine of opportunity that has helped lift some of its neighbors out of poverty and desperation. It is the initiative by Indonesia that allows U.S. assistance to make a difference.

In the Western Hemisphere we have formed flexible coalitions with countries that share our priorities, particularly Mexico, Brazil, Canada, Chile, and Colombia. Together we will promote a truly democratic hemisphere where our integration advances security, prosperity, opportunity, and hope. We will work with regional institutions, such as the Summit of the Americas process, the Organization of American States (OAS), and the Defense Ministerial of the Americas for the benefit of the entire hemisphere.

Parts of Latin America confront regional conflict, especially arising from the violence of drug cartels and their accomplices. This conflict and unrestrained narcotics trafficking could imperil the health and security of the United States. Therefore we have developed an active strategy to help the Andean nations adjust their economies, enforce their laws, defeat terrorist organizations, and cut off the supply of drugs, while—as important—we work to reduce the demand for drugs in our own country.

In Colombia, we recognize the link between terrorist and extremist groups that challenge the security of the state and drug trafficking activities that help finance the operations of such groups. We are working to help Colombia defend its democratic institutions and defeat illegal armed groups of both the left and right by extending effective sovereignty over the entire national territory and provide basic security to the Colombian people.

In Africa, promise and opportunity sit side by side with disease, war, and desperate poverty. This threatens both a core value of the United States—preserving human dignity—and our strategic priority—combating global terror. American interests and American principles, therefore, lead in the same direction: we will work with others for an African continent that lives in liberty, peace, and growing prosperity. Together with our European allies, we must help strengthen Africa's fragile states, help build indigenous capability to secure porous borders, and help build up the law enforcement and intelligence infrastructure to deny havens for terrorists.

An ever more lethal environment exists in Africa as local civil wars spread beyond borders to create regional war zones. Forming coalitions of the willing and cooperative security arrangements are key to confronting these emerging transnational threats.

Africa's great size and diversity require a security strategy that focuses on bilateral engagement and builds coalitions of the willing. This Administration will focus on three interlocking strategies for the region:

- countries with major impact on their neighborhood such as South Africa, Nigeria, Kenya, and Ethiopia are anchors for regional engagement and require focused attention;

- coordination with European allies and international institutions is essential for constructive conflict mediation and successful peace operations; and

- Africa's capable reforming states and sub-regional organizations must be strengthened as the primary means to address transnational threats on a sustained basis.

Ultimately the path of political and economic freedom presents the surest route to progress in sub-Saharan Africa, where most wars are conflicts over material resources and political access often tragically waged on the basis of ethnic and religious difference. The transition to the African Union with its stated commitment to good governance and a common responsibility for democratic political systems offers opportunities to strengthen democracy on the continent.

V. PREVENT OUR ENEMIES FROM THREATENING US, OUR ALLIES, AND OUR FRIENDS WITH WEAPONS OF MASS DESTRUCTION

"The gravest danger to freedom lies at the crossroads of radicalism and technology. When the spread of chemical and biological and nuclear weapons, along with ballistic missile technology—when that occurs, even weak states and small groups could attain a catastrophic power to strike great nations. Our enemies have declared this very intention, and have been caught seeking these terrible weapons. They want the capability to blackmail us, or to harm us, or to harm our friends—and we will oppose them with all our power."

President Bush
West Point, New York
June 1, 2002

The nature of the Cold War threat required the United States—with our allies and friends—to emphasize deterrence of the enemy's use of force, producing a grim strategy of mutual assured destruction. With the collapse of the Soviet Union and the end of the Cold War, our security environment has undergone profound transformation.

Having moved from confrontation to cooperation as the hallmark of our relationship with Russia, the dividends are evident: an end to the balance of terror that divided us; an historic reduction in the nuclear arsenals on both sides; and cooperation in areas such as counterterrorism and missile defense that until recently were inconceivable.

But new deadly challenges have emerged from rogue states and terrorists. None of these contemporary threats rival the sheer destructive power that was arrayed against us by the Soviet Union. However, the nature and motivations of these new adversaries, their determination to obtain destructive powers hitherto available only to the world's strongest states, and the greater likelihood that they will use weapons of mass destruction against us, make today's security environment more complex and dangerous.

In the 1990s we witnessed the emergence of a small number of rogue states that, while different in important ways, share a number of attributes. These states:

- brutalize their own people and squander their national resources for the personal gain of the rulers;

- display no regard for international law, threaten their neighbors, and callously violate international treaties to which they are party;

- are determined to acquire weapons of mass destruction, along with other advanced military technology, to be used as threats or offensively to achieve the aggressive designs of these regimes;

- sponsor terrorism around the globe; and

- reject basic human values and hate the United States and everything for which it stands.

At the time of the Gulf War, we acquired irrefutable proof that Iraq's designs were not limited to the chemical weapons it had used against Iran and its own people, but also extended to the acquisition of nuclear weapons and biological agents. In the past decade North Korea has become the world's principal purveyor of ballistic missiles, and has tested increasingly capable missiles while developing its own WMD arsenal. Other rogue regimes seek nuclear, biological, and chemical weapons as well. These states' pursuit of, and global trade in, such weapons has become a looming threat to all nations.

We must be prepared to stop rogue states and their terrorist clients before they are able to threaten or use weapons of mass destruction against the United States and our allies and friends. Our response must take full advantage of strengthened alliances, the establishment of new partnerships with former adversaries, innovation in the use of military forces, modern technologies, including the development of an effective missile defense system, and increased emphasis on intelligence collection and analysis.

Our comprehensive strategy to combat WMD includes:

- *Proactive counterproliferation efforts.* We must deter and defend against the threat before it is unleashed. We must ensure that key capabilities—detection, active and passive defenses, and counterforce capabilities—are integrated into our defense transformation and our homeland security systems. Counterproliferation must also be integrated into the doctrine, training, and equipping of our forces and those of our allies to ensure that we can prevail in any conflict with WMD-armed adversaries.

- *Strengthened nonproliferation efforts to prevent rogue states and terrorists from acquiring the materials, technologies, and expertise necessary for weapons of mass destruction.* We will enhance diplomacy, arms control, multilateral export controls, and threat reduction assistance that impede states and terrorists seeking WMD, and when necessary, interdict enabling technologies and materials. We will continue to build coalitions to support these efforts, encouraging their increased political and financial support for nonproliferation and threat reduction programs. The recent G-8 agreement to commit up to $20 billion to a global partnership against proliferation marks a major step forward.

- *Effective consequence management to respond to the effects of WMD use, whether by terrorists or hostile states.* Minimizing the effects of WMD use against our people will help deter those who possess such weapons and dissuade those who seek to acquire them by persuading enemies that they cannot attain their desired ends. The United States must also be prepared to respond to the effects of WMD use against our forces abroad, and to help friends and allies if they are attacked.

It has taken almost a decade for us to comprehend the true nature of this new threat. Given the goals of rogue states and terrorists, the United States can no longer solely rely on a reactive posture as we have in the past. The inability to deter a potential attacker, the immediacy of today's threats, and the magnitude of potential harm that could be caused by our adversaries' choice of weapons, do not permit that option. We cannot let our enemies strike first.

In the Cold War, especially following the Cuban missile crisis, we faced a generally status quo, risk-averse adversary. Deterrence was an effective defense. But deterrence based only upon the threat of retaliation is less likely to work against leaders of rogue states more willing to take risks, gambling with the lives of their people, and the wealth of their nations.

- In the Cold War, weapons of mass destruction were considered weapons of last resort whose use risked the destruction of those who used them. Today, our enemies see weapons of mass destruction as weapons of choice. For rogue states these weapons are tools of intimidation and military aggression against their neighbors. These weapons may also allow these states to attempt to blackmail the United States and our allies to prevent us from deterring or repelling the aggressive behavior of rogue states. Such states also see these weapons as their best means of overcoming the conventional superiority of the United States.

- Traditional concepts of deterrence will not work against a terrorist enemy whose avowed tactics are wanton destruction and the targeting of innocents; whose so-called soldiers seek martyrdom in death and whose most potent protection is statelessness. The overlap between states that sponsor terror and those that pursue WMD compels us to action.

For centuries, international law recognized that nations need not suffer an attack before they can lawfully take action to defend themselves against forces that present an imminent danger of attack. Legal scholars and international jurists often conditioned the legitimacy of preemption on the existence of an imminent threat—most often a visible mobilization of armies, navies, and air forces preparing to attack.

We must adapt the concept of imminent threat to the capabilities and objectives of today's adversaries. Rogue states and terrorists do not seek to attack us using conventional means. They know such attacks would fail. Instead, they rely on acts of terror and, potentially, the use of weapons of mass destruction—weapons that can be easily concealed, delivered covertly, and used without warning.

The targets of these attacks are our military forces and our civilian population, in direct violation of one of the principal norms of the law of warfare. As was demonstrated by the losses on September 11, 2001, mass civilian casualties is the specific objective of terrorists and these losses would be exponentially more severe if terrorists acquired and used weapons of mass destruction.

The United States has long maintained the option of preemptive actions to counter a sufficient threat to our national security. The greater the threat, the greater is the risk of inaction—and the more compelling the case for taking anticipatory action to defend ourselves, even if uncertainty remains as to the time and place of the enemy's attack. To forestall or prevent such hostile acts by our adversaries, the United States will, if necessary, act preemptively.

The United States will not use force in all cases to preempt emerging threats, nor should nations use preemption as a pretext for aggression. Yet in an age where the enemies of civilization openly and actively seek the world's most destructive technologies, the United States cannot remain idle while dangers gather. We will always proceed deliberately, weighing the consequences of our actions. To support preemptive options, we will:

- build better, more integrated intelligence capabilities to provide timely, accurate information on threats, wherever they may emerge;

- coordinate closely with allies to form a common assessment of the most dangerous threats; and

- continue to transform our military forces to ensure our ability to conduct rapid and precise operations to achieve decisive results.

The purpose of our actions will always be to eliminate a specific threat to the United States or our allies and friends. The reasons for our actions will be clear, the force measured, and the cause just.

VI. IGNITE A NEW ERA OF GLOBAL ECONOMIC GROWTH THROUGH FREE MARKETS AND FREE TRADE

"When nations close their markets and opportunity is hoarded by a privileged few, no amount—no amount—of development aid is ever enough. When nations respect their people, open markets, invest in better health and education, every dollar of aid, every dollar of trade revenue and domestic capital is used more effectively."

President Bush
Monterrey, Mexico
March 22, 2002

A strong world economy enhances our national security by advancing prosperity and freedom in the rest of the world. Economic growth supported by free trade and free markets creates new jobs and higher incomes. It allows people to lift their lives out of poverty, spurs economic and legal reform, and the fight against corruption, and it reinforces the habits of liberty.

We will promote economic growth and economic freedom beyond America's shores. All governments are responsible for creating their own economic policies and responding to their own economic challenges. We will use our economic engagement with other countries to underscore the benefits of policies that generate higher productivity and sustained economic growth, including:

- pro-growth legal and regulatory policies to encourage business investment, innovation, and entrepreneurial activity;

- tax policies—particularly lower marginal tax rates—that improve incentives for work and investment;

- rule of law and intolerance of corruption so that people are confident that they will be able to enjoy the fruits of their economic endeavors;

- strong financial systems that allow capital to be put to its most efficient use;

- sound fiscal policies to support business activity;

- investments in health and education that improve the well-being and skills of the labor force and population as a whole; and

- free trade that provides new avenues for growth and fosters the diffusion of technologies and ideas that increase productivity and opportunity.

The lessons of history are clear: market economies, not command-and-control economies with the heavy hand of government, are the best way to promote prosperity and reduce poverty. Policies that further strengthen market incentives and market institutions are relevant for all economies—industrialized countries, emerging markets, and the developing world.

A return to strong economic growth in Europe and Japan is vital to U.S. national security interests. We want our allies to have strong economies for their own sake, for the sake of the global economy, and for the sake of global security. European efforts to remove structural barriers in their economies are particularly important in this regard, as are Japan's efforts to end deflation and address the problems of non-performing loans in the Japanese banking system. We will continue to use our regular consultations with Japan and our European partners—including through the Group of Seven (G-7)—to discuss policies they are adopting to promote growth in their economies and support higher global economic growth.

Improving stability in emerging markets is also key to global economic growth. International flows of investment capital are needed to expand the productive potential of these economies. These flows allow emerging markets and developing countries to make the investments that raise living standards and reduce poverty. Our long-term objective should be a world in which all countries have investment-grade credit ratings that allow them access to international capital markets and to invest in their future.

We are committed to policies that will help emerging markets achieve access to larger capital flows at lower cost. To this end, we will continue to pursue reforms aimed at reducing uncertainty in financial markets. We will work actively with other countries, the International Monetary Fund (IMF), and the private sector to implement the G-7 Action Plan negotiated earlier this year for preventing financial crises and more effectively resolving them when they occur.

The best way to deal with financial crises is to prevent them from occurring, and we have encouraged the IMF to improve its efforts doing so. We will continue to work with the IMF to streamline the policy conditions for its lending and to focus its lending strategy on achieving economic growth through sound fiscal and monetary policy, exchange rate policy, and financial sector policy.

The concept of "free trade" arose as a moral principle even before it became a pillar of economics. If you can make something that others value, you should be able to sell it to them. If others make something that you value, you should be able to buy it. This is real freedom, the freedom for a person—or a nation—to make a living. To promote free trade, the Unites States has developed a comprehensive strategy:

- *Seize the global initiative.* The new global trade negotiations we helped launch at Doha in November 2001 will have an ambitious agenda, especially in agriculture, manufacturing, and services, targeted for completion in 2005. The United States has led the way in completing the accession of China and a democratic Taiwan to the World Trade Organization. We will assist Russia's preparations to join the WTO.

- *Press regional initiatives.* The United States and other democracies in the Western Hemisphere have agreed to create the Free Trade Area of the Americas, targeted for completion in 2005. This year the United States will advocate market-access negotiations with its partners, targeted on agriculture, industrial goods, services, investment, and government procurement. We will also offer more opportunity to the poorest continent, Africa, starting with full use of the preferences allowed in the African Growth and Opportunity Act, and leading to free trade.

- *Move ahead with bilateral free trade agreements.* Building on the free trade agreement with Jordan enacted in 2001, the Administration will work this year to complete free trade agreements with Chile and Singapore. Our aim is to achieve free trade agreements with a mix of developed and developing countries in all regions of the world. Initially, Central America, Southern Africa, Morocco, and Australia will be our principal focal points.

- *Renew the executive-congressional partnership.* Every administration's trade strategy depends on a productive partnership with Congress. After a gap of 8 years, the Administration reestablished majority support in the Congress for trade liberalization by passing Trade Promotion Authority and the other market opening measures for developing countries in the Trade Act of 2002. This Administration will work with Congress to enact new bilateral, regional, and global trade agreements that will be concluded under the recently passed Trade Promotion Authority.

- *Promote the connection between trade and development.* Trade policies can help developing countries strengthen property rights, competition, the rule of law, investment, the spread of knowledge, open societies, the efficient allocation of resources, and regional integration—all leading to growth, opportunity, and confidence in developing countries. The United States is implementing The Africa Growth and Opportunity Act to provide market access for nearly all goods produced in the 35 countries of sub-Saharan Africa. We will make more use of this act and its equivalent for the Caribbean Basin and continue to work with multilateral and regional institutions to help poorer countries take advantage of these opportunities. Beyond market access, the most important area where trade intersects with poverty is in public health. We will ensure that the WTO intellectual property rules are flexible enough to allow developing nations to gain access to critical medicines for extraordinary dangers like HIV/AIDS, tuberculosis, and malaria.

• *Enforce trade agreements and laws against unfair practices.* Commerce depends on the rule of law; international trade depends on enforceable agreements. Our top priorities are to resolve ongoing disputes with the European Union, Canada, and Mexico and to make a global effort to address new technology, science, and health regulations that needlessly impede farm exports and improved agriculture. Laws against unfair trade practices are often abused, but the international community must be able to address genuine concerns about government subsidies and dumping. International industrial espionage which undermines fair competition must be detected and deterred.

• *Help domestic industries and workers adjust.* There is a sound statutory framework for these transitional safeguards which we have used in the agricultural sector and which we are using this year to help the American steel industry. The benefits of free trade depend upon the enforcement of fair trading practices. These safeguards help ensure that the benefits of free trade do not come at the expense of American workers. Trade adjustment assistance will help workers adapt to the change and dynamism of open markets.

• *Protect the environment and workers.* The United States must foster economic growth in ways that will provide a better life along with widening prosperity. We will incorporate labor and environmental concerns into U.S. trade negotiations, creating a healthy "network" between multilateral environmental agreements with the WTO, and use the International Labor Organization, trade preference programs, and trade talks to improve working conditions in conjunction with freer trade.

• *Enhance energy security.* We will strengthen our own energy security and the shared prosperity of the global economy by working with our allies, trading partners, and energy producers to expand the sources and types of global energy supplied, especially in the Western Hemisphere, Africa, Central Asia, and the Caspian region. We will also continue to work with our partners to develop cleaner and more energy efficient technologies.

Economic growth should be accompanied by global efforts to stabilize greenhouse gas concentrations associated with this growth, containing them at a level that prevents dangerous human interference with the global climate. Our overall objective is to reduce America's greenhouse gas emissions relative to the size of our economy, cutting such emissions per unit of economic activity by 18 percent over the next 10 years, by the year 2012. Our strategies for attaining this goal will be to:

- remain committed to the basic U.N. Framework Convention for international cooperation;

- obtain agreements with key industries to cut emissions of some of the most potent greenhouse gases and give transferable credits to companies that can show real cuts;

- develop improved standards for measuring and registering emission reductions;

- promote renewable energy production and clean coal technology, as well as nuclear power—which produces no greenhouse gas emissions, while also improving fuel economy for U.S. cars and trucks;

- increase spending on research and new conservation technologies, to a total of $4.5 billion—the largest sum being spent on climate change by any country in the world and a $700 million increase over last year's budget; and

- assist developing countries, especially the major greenhouse gas emitters such as China and India, so that they will have the tools and resources to join this effort and be able to grow along a cleaner and better path.

VII. EXPAND THE CIRCLE OF DEVELOPMENT BY
OPENING SOCIETIES AND BUILDING THE INFRASTRUCTURE
OF DEMOCRACY

*"In World War II we fought to make the world safer,
then worked to rebuild it. As we wage war today to keep
the world safe from terror, we must also work to make the
world a better place for all its citizens."*

President Bush
Washington, D.C. (Inter-American Development Bank)
March 14, 2002

A world where some live in comfort and plenty while half of the human race lives on less than $2 a day is neither just nor stable. Including all of the world's poor in an expanding circle of development—and opportunity—is a moral imperative and one of the top priorities of U.S. international policy.

Decades of massive development assistance have failed to spur economic growth in the poorest countries. Worse, development aid has often served to prop up failed policies, relieving the pressure for reform and perpetuating misery. Results of aid are typically measured in dollars spent by donors, not in the rates of growth and poverty reduction achieved by recipients. These are the indicators of a failed strategy.

Working with other nations, the United States is confronting this failure. We forged a new consensus at the U.N. Conference on Financing for Development in Monterrey that the objectives of assistance—and the strategies to achieve those objectives—must change.

This Administration's goal is to help unleash the productive potential of individuals in all nations. Sustained growth and poverty reduction is impossible without the right national policies. Where governments have implemented real policy changes, we will provide significant new levels of assistance. The United States and other developed countries should set an ambitious and specific target: to double the size of the world's poorest economies within a decade.

[125]

The United States Government will pursue these major strategies to achieve this goal:

- *Provide resources to aid countries that have met the challenge of national reform.* We propose a 50 percent increase in the core development assistance given by the United States. While continuing our present programs, including humanitarian assistance based on need alone, these billions of new dollars will form a new Millennium Challenge Account for projects in countries whose governments rule justly, invest in their people, and encourage economic freedom. Governments must fight corruption, respect basic human rights, embrace the rule of law, invest in health care and education, follow responsible economic policies, and enable entrepreneurship. The Millennium Challenge Account will reward countries that have demonstrated real policy change and challenge those that have not to implement reforms.

- *Improve the effectiveness of the World Bank and other development banks in raising living standards.* The United States is committed to a comprehensive reform agenda for making the World Bank and the other multilateral development banks more effective in improving the lives of the world's poor. We have reversed the downward trend in U.S. contributions and proposed an 18 percent increase in the U.S. contributions to the International Development Association (IDA)—the World Bank's fund for the poorest countries—and the African Development Fund. The key to raising living standards and reducing poverty around the world is increasing productivity growth, especially in the poorest countries. We will continue to press the multilateral development banks to focus on activities that increase economic productivity, such as improvements in education, health, rule of law, and private sector development. Every project, every loan, every grant must be judged by how much it will increase productivity growth in developing countries.

- *Insist upon measurable results to ensure that development assistance is actually making a difference in the lives of the world's poor.* When it comes to economic development, what really matters is that more children are getting a better education, more people have access to health care and clean water, or more workers can find jobs to make a better future for their families. We have a moral obligation to measure the success of our development assistance by whether it is delivering results. For this reason, we will continue to demand that our own development assistance as well as assistance from the multilateral development banks has measurable goals and concrete benchmarks for achieving those goals. Thanks to U.S. leadership, the recent IDA replenishment agreement will establish a monitoring and evaluation system that measures recipient countries' progress. For the first time, donors can link a portion of their contributions to IDA to the achievement of actual development results, and part of the U.S. contribution is linked in this way. We will strive to make sure that the World Bank and other multilateral development banks build on this progress so that a focus on results is an integral part of everything that these institutions do.

- *Increase the amount of development assistance that is provided in the form of grants instead of loans.* Greater use of results-based grants is the best way to help poor countries make productive investments, particularly in the social sectors, without saddling them with ever-larger debt burdens. As a result of U.S. leadership, the recent IDA agreement provided for significant increases in grant funding for the poorest countries for education, HIV/AIDS, health, nutrition, water, sanitation, and other human needs. Our goal is to build on that progress by increasing the use of grants at the other multilateral development banks. We will also challenge universities, nonprofits, and the private sector to match government efforts by using grants to support development projects that show results.

- *Open societies to commerce and investment.* Trade and investment are the real engines of economic growth. Even if government aid increases, most money for development must come from trade, domestic capital, and foreign investment. An effective strategy must try to expand these flows as well. Free markets and free trade are key priorities of our national security strategy.

- *Secure public health.* The scale of the public health crisis in poor countries is enormous. In countries afflicted by epidemics and pandemics like HIV/AIDS, malaria, and tuberculosis, growth and development will be threatened until these scourges can be contained. Resources from the developed world are necessary but will be effective only with honest governance, which supports prevention programs and provides effective local infrastructure. The United States has strongly backed the new global fund for HIV/AIDS organized by UN Secretary-General Kofi Annan and its focus on combining prevention with a broad strategy for treatment and care. The United States already contributes more than twice as much money to such efforts as the next largest donor. If the global fund demonstrates its promise, we will be ready to give even more.

- *Emphasize education.* Literacy and learning are the foundation of democracy and development. Only about 7 percent of World Bank resources are devoted to education. This proportion should grow. The United States will increase its own funding for education assistance by at least 20 percent with an emphasis on improving basic education and teacher training in Africa. The United States can also bring information technology to these societies, many of whose education systems have been devastated by HIV/AIDS.

- *Continue to aid agricultural development.* New technologies, including biotechnology, have enormous potential to improve crop yields in developing countries while using fewer pesticides and less water. Using sound science, the United States should help bring these benefits to the 800 million people, including 300 million children, who still suffer from hunger and malnutrition.

VIII. DEVELOP AGENDAS FOR COOPERATIVE ACTION WITH THE OTHER MAIN CENTERS OF GLOBAL POWER

"We have our best chance since the rise of the nation-state in the 17th century to build a world where the great powers compete in peace instead of prepare for war."

President Bush
West Point, New York
June 1, 2002

America will implement its strategies by organizing coalitions—as broad as practicable—of states able and willing to promote a balance of power that favors freedom. Effective coalition leadership requires clear priorities, an appreciation of others' interests, and consistent consultations among partners with a spirit of humility.

There is little of lasting consequence that the United States can accomplish in the world without the sustained cooperation of its allies and friends in Canada and Europe. Europe is also the seat of two of the strongest and most able international institutions in the world: the North Atlantic Treaty Organization (NATO), which has, since its inception, been the fulcrum of transatlantic and inter-European security, and the European Union (EU), our partner in opening world trade.

The attacks of September 11 were also an attack on NATO, as NATO itself recognized when it invoked its Article V self-defense clause for the first time. NATO's core mission—collective defense of the transatlantic alliance of democracies—remains, but NATO must develop new structures and capabilities to carry out that mission under new circumstances. NATO must build a capability to field, at short notice, highly mobile, specially trained forces whenever they are needed to respond to a threat against any member of the alliance.

The alliance must be able to act wherever our interests are threatened, creating coalitions under NATO's own mandate, as well as contributing to mission-based coalitions. To achieve this, we must:

- expand NATO's membership to those democratic nations willing and able to share the burden of defending and advancing our common interests;

- ensure that the military forces of NATO nations have appropriate combat contributions to make in coalition warfare;

- develop planning processes to enable those contributions to become effective multinational fighting forces;

- take advantage of the technological opportunities and economies of scale in our defense spending to transform NATO military forces so that they dominate potential aggressors and diminish our vulnerabilities;

- streamline and increase the flexibility of command structures to meet new operational demands and the associated requirements of training, integrating, and experimenting with new force configurations; and

- maintain the ability to work and fight together as allies even as we take the necessary steps to transform and modernize our forces.

If NATO succeeds in enacting these changes, the rewards will be a partnership as central to the security and interests of its member states as was the case during the Cold War. We will sustain a common perspective on the threats to our societies and improve our ability to take common action in defense of our nations and their interests. At the same time, we welcome our European allies' efforts to forge a greater foreign policy and defense identity with the EU, and commit ourselves to close consultations to ensure that these developments work with NATO. We cannot afford to lose this opportunity to better prepare the family of transatlantic democracies for the challenges to come.

The attacks of September 11 energized America's Asian alliances. Australia invoked the ANZUS Treaty to declare the September 11 was an attack on Australia itself, following that historic decision with the dispatch of some of the world's finest combat forces for Operation Enduring Freedom. Japan and the Republic of

Korea provided unprecedented levels of military logistical support within weeks of the terrorist attack. We have deepened cooperation on counterterrorism with our alliance partners in Thailand and the Philippines and received invaluable assistance from close friends like Singapore and New Zealand.

The war against terrorism has proven that America's alliances in Asia not only underpin regional peace and stability, but are flexible and ready to deal with new challenges. To enhance our Asian alliances and friendships, we will:

- look to Japan to continue forging a leading role in regional and global affairs based on our common interests, our common values, and our close defense and diplomatic cooperation;

- work with South Korea to maintain vigilance towards the North while preparing our alliance to make contributions to the broader stability of the region over the longer term;

- build on 50 years of U.S.-Australian alliance cooperation as we continue working together to resolve regional and global problems—as we have so many times from the Battle of the Coral Sea to Tora Bora;

- maintain forces in the region that reflect our commitments to our allies, our requirements, our technological advances, and the strategic environment; and

- build on stability provided by these alliances, as well as with institutions such as ASEAN and the Asia-Pacific Economic Cooperation forum, to develop a mix of regional and bilateral strategies to manage change in this dynamic region.

We are attentive to the possible renewal of old patterns of great power competition. Several potential great powers are now in the midst of internal transition—most importantly Russia, India, and China. In all three cases, recent developments have encouraged our hope that a truly global consensus about basic principles is slowly taking shape.

With Russia, we are already building a new strategic relationship based on a central reality of the twenty-first century: the United States and Russia are no longer strategic adversaries. The Moscow Treaty on Strategic Reductions is emblematic of this new reality and reflects a critical change in Russian thinking that promises to lead to productive, long-term relations with the Euro-Atlantic community and the United States. Russia's top leaders have a realistic assessment of their country's current weakness and the policies—internal and external—needed to reverse those weaknesses. They understand, increasingly, that Cold War approaches do not serve their national interests and that Russian and American strategic interests overlap in many areas.

United States policy seeks to use this turn in Russian thinking to refocus our relationship on emerging and potential common interests and challenges. We are broadening our already extensive cooperation in the global war on terrorism. We are facilitating Russia's entry into the World Trade Organization, without lowering standards for accession, to promote beneficial bilateral trade and investment relations. We have created the NATO-Russia Council with the goal of deepening security cooperation among Russia, our European allies, and ourselves. We will continue to bolster the independence and stability of the states of the former Soviet Union in the belief that a prosperous and stable neighborhood will reinforce Russia's growing commitment to integration into the Euro-Atlantic community.

At the same time, we are realistic about the differences that still divide us from Russia and about the time and effort it will take to build an enduring strategic partnership. Lingering distrust of our motives and policies by key Russian elites slows improvement in our relations. Russia's uneven commitment to the basic values of free-market democracy and dubious record in combating the proliferation of weapons of mass destruction remain matters of great concern. Russia's very weakness limits the opportunities for cooperation. Nevertheless, those opportunities are vastly greater now than in recent years—or even decades.

The United States has undertaken a transformation in its bilateral relationship with India based on a conviction that U.S. interests require a strong relationship with India. We are the two largest democracies, committed to political freedom protected by representative government. India is moving toward greater economic freedom as well. We have a common interest in the free flow of commerce, including through the vital sea lanes of the Indian Ocean. Finally, we share an interest in fighting terrorism and in creating a strategically stable Asia.

Differences remain, including over the development of India's nuclear and missile programs, and the pace of India's economic reforms. But while in the past these concerns may have dominated our thinking about India, today we start with a view of India as a growing world power with which we have common strategic interests. Through a strong partnership with India, we can best address any differences and shape a dynamic future.

The United States relationship with China is an important part of our strategy to promote a stable, peaceful, and prosperous Asia-Pacific region. We welcome the emergence of a strong, peaceful, and prosperous China. The democratic development of China is crucial to that future. Yet, a quarter century after beginning the process of shedding the worst features of the Communist legacy, China's leaders have not yet made the next series of fundamental choices about the character of their state. In pursuing advanced military capabilities that can threaten its neighbors in the Asia-Pacific region, China is following an outdated path that, in the end, will hamper its own pursuit of national greatness. In time, China will find that social and political freedom is the only source of that greatness.

The United States seeks a constructive relationship with a changing China. We already cooperate well where our interests overlap, including the current war on terrorism and in promoting stability on the Korean peninsula. Likewise, we have coordinated on the future of Afghanistan and have initiated a comprehensive dialogue on counterterrorism and similar transitional concerns. Shared health and environmental threats, such as the spread of HIV/AIDS, challenge us to promote jointly the welfare of our citizens.

Addressing these transnational threats will challenge China to become more open with information, promote the development of civil society, and enhance individual human rights. China has begun to take the road to political openness, permitting many personal freedoms and conducting village-level elections, yet remains strongly committed to national one-party rule by the Communist Party. To make that nation truly accountable to its citizens' needs and aspirations, however, much work remains to be done. Only by allowing the Chinese people to think, assemble, and worship freely can China reach its full potential.

Our important trade relationship will benefit from China's entry into the World Trade Organization, which will create more export opportunities and ultimately more jobs for American farmers, workers, and companies. China is our fourth largest trading partner, with over $100 billion in annual two-way trade. The power of market principles and the WTO's requirements for transparency and accountability will advance openness and the rule of law in China to help establish basic protections for commerce and for citizens. There are, however, other areas in which we have profound disagreements. Our commitment to the self-defense of Taiwan under the Taiwan Relations Act is one. Human rights is another. We expect China to adhere to its nonproliferation commitments. We will work to narrow differences where they exist, but not allow them to preclude cooperation where we agree.

The events of September 11, 2001, fundamentally changed the context for relations between the United States and other main centers of global power, and opened vast, new opportunities. With our long-standing allies in Europe and Asia, and with leaders in Russia, India, and China, we must develop active agendas of cooperation lest these relationships become routine and unproductive.

Every agency of the United States Government shares the challenge. We can build fruitful habits of consultation, quiet argument, sober analysis, and common action. In the long-term, these are the practices that will sustain the supremacy of our common principles and keep open the path of progress.

IX. TRANSFORM AMERICA'S NATIONAL SECURITY INSTITUTIONS TO MEET THE CHALLENGES AND OPPORTUNITIES OF THE TWENTY-FIRST CENTURY

"Terrorists attacked a symbol of American prosperity. They did not touch its source. America is successful because of the hard work, creativity, and enterprise of our people."

President Bush
Washington, D.C. (Joint Session of Congress)
September 20, 2001

The major institutions of American national security were designed in a different era to meet different requirements. All of them must be transformed.

It is time to reaffirm the essential role of American military strength. We must build and maintain our defenses beyond challenge. Our military's highest priority is to defend the United States. To do so effectively, our military must:

- assure our allies and friends;

- dissuade future military competition;

- deter threats against U.S. interests, allies, and friends; and

- decisively defeat any adversary if deterrence fails.

The unparalleled strength of the United States armed forces and their forward presence have maintained the peace in some of the world's most strategically vital regions. However, the threats and enemies we must confront have changed, and so must our forces. A military structured to deter massive Cold War–era armies must be transformed to focus more on how an adversary might fight rather than where and when a war might occur. We will channel our energies to overcome a host of operational challenges.

The presence of American forces overseas is one of the most profound symbols of the U.S. commitments to allies and friends. Through our willingness to use force in our own defense and in defense of others, the United States demonstrates its resolve to maintain a balance of power that favors freedom. To contend with uncertainty and to meet the many security challenges we face, the United States will require bases and stations within and beyond Western Europe and Northeast Asia, as well as temporary access arrangements for the long-distance deployment of U.S. forces.

Before the war in Afghanistan, that area was low on the list of major planning contingencies. Yet, in a very short time, we had to operate across the length and breadth of that remote nation, using every branch of the armed forces. We must prepare for more such deployments by developing assets such as advanced remote sensing, long-range precision strike capabilities, and transformed maneuver and expeditionary forces. This broad portfolio of military capabilities must also include the ability to defend the homeland, conduct information operations, ensure U.S. access to distant theaters, and protect critical U.S. infrastructure and assets in outer space.

Innovation within the armed forces will rest on experimentation with new approaches to warfare, strengthening joint operations, exploiting U.S. intelligence advantages, and taking full advantage of science and technology. We must also transform the way the Department of Defense is run, especially in financial management and recruitment and retention. Finally, while maintaining near-term readiness and the ability to fight the war on terrorism, the goal must be to provide the President with a wider range of military options to discourage aggression or any form of coercion against the United States, our allies, and our friends.

We know from history that deterrence can fail; and we know from experience that some enemies cannot be deterred. The United States must and will maintain the capability to defeat any attempt by an enemy—whether a state or non-state actor—to impose its will on the United States, our allies, or our friends. We will maintain the forces sufficient to support our obligations, and to defend freedom. Our forces will be strong enough to dissuade potential adversaries from pursuing a military build-up in hopes of surpassing, or equaling, the power of the United States.

Intelligence—and how we use it—is our first line of defense against terrorists and the threat posed by hostile states. Designed around the priority of gathering enormous information about a massive, fixed object—the Soviet bloc—the intelligence community is coping with the challenge of following a far more complex and elusive set of targets.

We must transform our intelligence capabilities and build new ones to keep pace with the nature of these threats. Intelligence must be appropriately integrated with our defense and law enforcement systems and coordinated with our allies and friends. We need to protect the capabilities we have so that we do not arm our enemies with the knowledge of how best to surprise us. Those who would harm us also seek the benefit of surprise to limit our prevention and response options and to maximize injury.

We must strengthen intelligence warning and analysis to provide integrated threat assessments for national and homeland security. Since the threats inspired by foreign governments and groups may be conducted inside the United States, we must also ensure the proper fusion of information between intelligence and law enforcement.

Initiatives in this area will include:

- strengthening the authority of the Director of Central Intelligence to lead the development and actions of the Nation's foreign intelligence capabilities;

- establishing a new framework for intelligence warning that provides seamless and integrated warning across the spectrum of threats facing the nation and our allies;

- continuing to develop new methods of collecting information to sustain our intelligence advantage;

- investing in future capabilities while working to protect them through a more vigorous effort to prevent the compromise of intelligence capabilities; and

- collecting intelligence against the terrorist danger across the government with all-source analysis.

As the United States Government relies on the armed forces to defend America's interests, it must rely on diplomacy to interact with other nations. We will ensure that the Department of State receives funding sufficient to ensure the success of American diplomacy. The State Department takes the lead in managing our bilateral relationships with other governments. And in this new era, its people and institutions must be able to interact equally adroitly with non-governmental organizations and international institutions. Officials trained mainly in international politics must also extend their reach to understand complex issues of domestic governance around the world, including public health, education, law enforcement, the judiciary, and public diplomacy.

Our diplomats serve at the front line of complex negotiations, civil wars, and other humanitarian catastrophes. As humanitarian relief requirements are better understood, we must also be able to help build police forces, court systems, and legal codes, local and provincial government institutions, and electoral systems. Effective international cooperation is needed to accomplish these goals, backed by American readiness to play our part.

Just as our diplomatic institutions must adapt so that we can reach out to others, we also need a different and more comprehensive approach to public information efforts that can help people around the world learn about and understand America. The war on terrorism is not a clash of civilizations. It does, however, reveal the clash inside a civilization, a battle for the future of the Muslim world. This is a struggle of ideas and this is an area where America must excel.

We will take the actions necessary to ensure that our efforts to meet our global security commitments and protect Americans are not impaired by the potential for investigations, inquiry, or prosecution by the International Criminal Court (ICC), whose jurisdiction does not extend to Americans and which we do not accept. We will work together with other nations to avoid complications in our military operations and cooperation, through such mechanisms as multilateral and bilateral agreements that will protect U.S. nationals from the ICC. We will implement fully the American Servicemembers Protection Act, whose provisions are intended to ensure and enhance the protection of U.S. personnel and officials.

We will make hard choices in the coming year and beyond to ensure the right level and allocation of government spending on national security. The United States Government must strengthen its defenses to win this war. At home, our most important priority is to protect the homeland for the American people.

Today, the distinction between domestic and foreign affairs is diminishing. In a globalized world, events beyond America's borders have a greater impact inside them. Our society must be open to people, ideas, and goods from across the globe. The characteristics we most cherish—our freedom, our cities, our systems of movement, and modern life—are vulnerable to terrorism. This vulnerability will persist long after we bring to justice those responsible for the September 11 attacks. As time passes, individuals may gain access to means of destruction that until now could be wielded only by armies, fleets, and squadrons. This is a new condition of life. We will adjust to it and thrive—in spite of it.

In exercising our leadership, we will respect the values, judgment, and interests of our friends and partners. Still, we will be prepared to act apart when our interests and unique responsibilities require. When we disagree on particulars, we will explain forthrightly the grounds for our concerns and strive to forge viable alternatives. We will not allow such disagreements to obscure our determination to secure together, with our allies and our friends, our shared fundamental interests and values.

Ultimately, the foundation of American strength is at home. It is in the skills of our people, the dynamism of our economy, and the resilience of our institutions. A diverse, modern society has inherent, ambitious, entrepreneurial energy. Our strength comes from what we do with that energy. That is where our national security begins.

APPENDIX B: NSPD-17/HSPD-4: NATIONAL STRATEGY TO COMBAT WEAPONS OF MASS DESTRUCTION, DECEMBER 2002

"The gravest danger our Nation faces lies at the crossroads of radicalism and technology. Our enemies have openly declared that they are seeking weapons of mass destruction, and evidence indicates that they are doing so with determination. The United States will not allow these efforts to succeed. . . . History will judge harshly those who saw this coming danger but failed to act. In the new world we have entered, the only path to peace and security is the path of action."

President Bush
The National Security Strategy
of the United States of America
September 17, 2002

INTRODUCTION

Weapons of mass destruction (WMD)—nuclear, biological, and chemical—in the possession of hostile states and terrorists represent one of the greatest security challenges facing the United States. We must pursue a comprehensive strategy to counter this threat in all of its dimensions.

An effective strategy for countering WMD, including their use and further proliferation, is an integral component of the National Security Strategy of the United States of America. As with the war on terrorism, our strategy for homeland security, and our new concept of deterrence, the U.S. approach to combat WMD represents a fundamental change from the past. To succeed, we must take full advantage of today's opportunities, including the application of new technologies, increased emphasis on intelligence collection and analysis, the strengthening of alliance relationships, and the establishment of new partnerships with former adversaries.

Weapons of mass destruction could enable adversaries to inflict massive harm on the United States, our military forces at home and abroad, and our friends and allies. Some states, including several that have supported and continue to support terrorism, already possess WMD and are seeking even greater capabilities, as tools of coercion and intimidation. For them, these are not weapons of last resort, but militarily useful weapons of choice intended to overcome our nation's advantages in conventional forces and to deter us from responding to aggression against our friends and allies in regions of vital interest. In addition, terrorist groups are seeking to acquire WMD with the stated purpose of killing large numbers of our people and those of friends and allies—without compunction and without warning.

We will not permit the world's most dangerous regimes and terrorists to threaten us with the world's most destructive weapons. We must accord the highest priority to the protection of the United States, our forces, and our friends and allies from the existing and growing WMD threat.

PILLARS OF OUR NATIONAL STRATEGY

Our National Strategy to Combat Weapons of Mass Destruction has three principal pillars:

Counterproliferation to Combat WMD Use
The possession and increased likelihood of use of WMD by hostile states and terrorists are realities of the contemporary security environment. It is therefore critical that the U.S. military and appropriate civilian agencies be prepared to deter and defend against the full range of possible WMD employment scenarios. We will ensure that all needed capabilities to combat WMD are fully integrated into the emerging defense transformation plan and into our homeland security posture. Counterproliferation will also be fully integrated into the basic doctrine, training, and

equipping of all forces, in order to ensure that they can sustain operations to decisively defeat WMD-armed adversaries.

Strengthened Nonproliferation to Combat WMD Proliferation
The United States, our friends and allies, and the broader international community must undertake every effort to prevent states and terrorists from acquiring WMD and missiles. We must enhance traditional measures—diplomacy, arms control, multilateral agreements, threat reduction assistance, and export controls—that seek to dissuade or impede proliferant states and terrorist networks, as well as to slow and make more costly their access to sensitive technologies, material, and expertise. We must ensure compliance with relevant international agreements, including the Nuclear Nonproliferation Treaty (NPT), the Chemical Weapons Convention (CWC), and the Biological Weapons Convention (BWC). The United States will continue to work with other states to improve their capability to prevent unauthorized transfers of WMD and missile technology, expertise, and material. We will identify and pursue new methods of prevention, such as national criminalization of proliferation activities and expanded safety and security measures.

Consequence Management to Respond to WMD Use
Finally, the United States must be prepared to respond to the use of WMD against our citizens, our military forces, and those of friends and allies. We will develop and maintain the capability to reduce to the extent possible the potentially horrific consequences of WMD attacks at home and abroad.

The three pillars of the U.S. national strategy to combat WMD are seamless elements of a comprehensive approach. Serving to integrate the pillars are four cross-cutting enabling functions that need to be pursued on a priority basis: intelligence collection and analysis on WMD, delivery systems, and related technologies; research and development to improve our ability to respond to evolving threats; bilateral and multilateral cooperation; and targeted strategies against hostile states and terrorists.

COUNTERPROLIFERATION

We know from experience that we cannot always be successful in preventing and containing the proliferation of WMD to hostile states and terrorists. Therefore, U.S. military and appropriate civilian agencies must possess the full range of operational capabilities to counter the threat and use of WMD by states and terrorists against the United States, our military forces, and friends and allies.

Interdiction

Effective interdiction is a critical part of the U.S. strategy to combat WMD and their delivery means. We must enhance the capabilities of our military, intelligence, technical, and law enforcement communities to prevent the movement of WMD materials, technology, and expertise to hostile states and terrorist organizations.

Deterrence

Today's threats are far more diverse and less predictable than those of the past. States hostile to the United States and to our friends and allies have demonstrated their willingness to take high risks to achieve their goals, and are aggressively pursuing WMD and their means of delivery as critical tools in this effort. As a consequence, we require new methods of deterrence. A strong declaratory policy and effective military forces are essential elements of our contemporary deterrent posture, along with the full range of political tools to persuade potential adversaries not to seek or use WMD. The United States will continue to make clear that it reserves the right to respond with overwhelming force—including through resort to all of our options—to the use of WMD against the United States, our forces abroad, and friends and allies.

In addition to our conventional and nuclear response and defense capabilities, our overall deterrent posture against WMD threats is reinforced by effective intelligence, surveillance, interdiction, and domestic law enforcement capabilities. Such combined capabilities enhance deterrence both by devaluing an adversary's

WMD and missiles, and by posing the prospect of an over-whelming response to any use of such weapons.

Defense and Mitigation

Because deterrence may not succeed, and because of the poten-tially devastating consequences of WMD use against our forces and civilian population, U.S. military forces and appropriate civil-ian agencies must have the capability to defend against WMD-armed adversaries, including in appropriate cases through preemptive measures. This requires capabilities to detect and destroy an adversary's WMD assets before these weapons are used. In addi-tion, robust active and passive defenses and mitigation measures must be in place to enable U.S. military forces and appropriate civil-ian agencies to accomplish their missions, and to assist friends and allies when WMD are used.

Active defenses disrupt, disable, or destroy WMD en route to their targets. Active defenses include vigorous air defense and effec-tive missile defenses against today's threats. Passive defenses must be tailored to the unique characteristics of the various forms of WMD. The United States must also have the ability rapidly and effectively to mitigate the effects of a WMD attack against our deployed forces.

Our approach to defend against biological threats has long been based on our approach to chemical threats, despite the fundamental differences between these weapons. The United States is devel-oping a new approach to provide us and our friends and allies with an effective defense against biological weapons.

Finally, U.S. military forces and domestic law enforcement agencies as appropriate must stand ready to respond against the source of any WMD attack. The primary objective of a response is to disrupt an imminent attack or an attack in progress, and elim-inate the threat of future attacks. As with deterrence and prevention, an effective response requires rapid attribution and robust strike capability. We must accelerate efforts to field new capabilities to defeat WMD-related assets. The United States needs to be pre-pared to conduct post-conflict operations to destroy or disman-tle any residual WMD capabilities of the hostile state or terrorist network. An effective U.S. response not only will eliminate the source of a WMD attack but will also have a powerful deterrent effect upon other adversaries that possess or seek WMD or missiles.

NONPROLIFERATION

Active Nonproliferation Diplomacy
The United States will actively employ diplomatic approaches in bilateral and multilateral settings in pursuit of our nonproliferation goals. We must dissuade supplier states from cooperating with proliferant states and induce proliferant states to end their WMD and missile programs. We will hold countries responsible for complying with their commitments. In addition, we will continue to build coalitions to support our efforts, as well as to seek their increased support for nonproliferation and threat reduction cooperation programs. However, should our wide-ranging nonproliferation efforts fail, we must have available the full range of operational capabilities necessary to defend against the possible employment of WMD.

Multilateral Regimes
Existing nonproliferation and arms control regimes play an important role in our overall strategy. The United States will support those regimes that are currently in force, and work to improve the effectiveness of, and compliance with, those regimes. Consistent with other policy priorities, we will also promote new agreements and arrangements that serve our nonproliferation goals. Overall, we seek to cultivate an international environment that is more conducive to nonproliferation. Our efforts will include:

- Nuclear
    - Strengthening of the Nuclear Nonproliferation Treaty and International Atomic Energy Agency (IAEA), including through ratification of an IAEA Additional Protocol by all NPT states parties, assurances that all states put in

place full-scope IAEA safeguards agreements, and appropriate increases in funding for the Agency;

- Negotiating a Fissile Material Cut-Off Treaty that advances U.S. security interests; and

- Strengthening the Nuclear Suppliers Group and Zangger Committee.

- Chemical and Biological
  - Effective functioning of the Organization for the Prohibition of Chemical Weapons;

  - Identification and promotion of constructive and realistic measures to strengthen the BWC and thereby to help meet the biological weapons threat; and

  - Strengthening of the Australia Group.

- Missile
  - Strengthening the Missile Technology Control Regime (MTCR), including through support for universal adherence to the International Code of Conduct Against Ballistic Missile Proliferation.

Nonproliferation and Threat Reduction Cooperation
The United States pursues a wide range of programs, including the Nunn-Lugar program, designed to address the proliferation threat stemming from the large quantities of Soviet-legacy WMD and missile-related expertise and materials. Maintaining an extensive and efficient set of nonproliferation and threat reduction assistance programs to Russia and other former Soviet states is a high priority. We will also continue to encourage friends and allies to increase their contributions to these programs, particularly through the G-8 Global Partnership Against the Spread of Weapons and Materials of Mass Destruction. In addition, we will work with other states to improve the security of their WMD-related materials.

Controls on Nuclear Materials

In addition to programs with former Soviet states to reduce fissile material and improve the security of that which remains, the United States will continue to discourage the worldwide accumulation of separated plutonium and to minimize the use of highly-enriched uranium. As outlined in the National Energy Policy, the United States will work in collaboration with international partners to develop recycle and fuel treatment technologies that are cleaner, more efficient, less waste-intensive, and more proliferation-resistant.

U.S. Export Controls

We must ensure that the implementation of U.S. export controls furthers our nonproliferation and other national security goals, while recognizing the realities that American businesses face in the increasingly globalized marketplace.

We will work to update and strengthen export controls using existing authorities. We also seek new legislation to improve the ability of our export control system to give full weight to both nonproliferation objectives and commercial interests. Our overall goal is to focus our resources on truly sensitive exports to hostile states or those that engage in onward proliferation, while removing unnecessary barriers in the global marketplace.

Nonproliferation Sanctions

Sanctions can be a valuable component of our overall strategy against WMD proliferation. At times, however, sanctions have proven inflexible and ineffective. We will develop a comprehensive sanctions policy to better integrate sanctions into our overall strategy and work with Congress to consolidate and modify existing sanctions legislation.

WMD CONSEQUENCE MANAGEMENT

Defending the American homeland is the most basic responsibility of our government. As part of our defense, the United States must be fully prepared to respond to the consequences of WMD use on our soil, whether by hostile states or by terrorists. We must also be prepared to respond to the effects of WMD use against our forces deployed abroad, and to assist friends and allies.

The National Strategy for Homeland Security discusses U.S. Government programs to deal with the consequences of the use of a chemical, biological, radiological, or nuclear weapon in the United States. A number of these programs offer training, planning, and assistance to state and local governments. To maximize their effectiveness, these efforts need to be integrated and comprehensive. Our first responders must have the full range of protective, medical, and remediation tools to identify, assess, and respond rapidly to a WMD event on our territory.

The White House Office of Homeland Security will coordinate all federal efforts to prepare for and mitigate the consequences of terrorist attacks within the United States, including those involving WMD. The Office of Homeland Security will also work closely with state and local governments to ensure their planning, training, and equipment requirements are addressed. These issues, including the roles of the Department of Homeland Security, are addressed in detail in the National Strategy for Homeland Security.

The National Security Council's Office of Combating Terrorism coordinates and helps improve U.S. efforts to respond to and manage the recovery from terrorist attacks outside the United States. In cooperation with the Office of Combating Terrorism, the Department of State coordinates interagency efforts to work with our friends and allies to develop their own emergency preparedness and consequence management capabilities.

INTEGRATING THE PILLARS

Several critical enabling functions serve to integrate the three pillars—counterproliferation, nonproliferation, and consequence management—of the U.S. National Strategy to Combat WMD.

Improved Intelligence Collection and Analysis
A more accurate and complete understanding of the full range of WMD threats is, and will remain, among the highest U.S. intelligence priorities, to enable us to prevent proliferation, and to deter or defend against those who would use those capabilities against us. Improving our ability to obtain timely and accurate knowledge of adversaries' offensive and defensive capabilities, plans, and intentions is key to developing effective counter- and nonproliferation policies and capabilities. Particular emphasis must be accorded to improving: intelligence regarding WMD-related facilities and activities; interaction among U.S. intelligence, law enforcement, and military agencies; and intelligence cooperation with friends and allies.

Research and Development
The United States has a critical need for cutting-edge technology that can quickly and effectively detect, analyze, facilitate interdiction of, defend against, defeat, and mitigate the consequences of WMD. Numerous U.S. Government departments and agencies are currently engaged in the essential research and development to support our overall strategy against WMD proliferation.

The new Counterproliferation Technology Coordination Committee, consisting of senior representatives from all concerned agencies, will act to improve interagency coordination of U.S. Government counterproliferation research and development efforts. The Committee will assist in identifying priorities, gaps, and overlaps in existing programs and in examining options for future investment strategies.

Strengthened International Cooperation
WMD represent a threat not just to the United States, but also to our friends and allies and the broader international community. For this reason, it is vital that we work closely with like-minded countries on all elements of our comprehensive proliferation strategy.

Targeted Strategies against Proliferants

All elements of the overall U.S. strategy to combat WMD must be brought to bear in targeted strategies against supplier and recipient states of WMD proliferation concern, as well as against terrorist groups which seek to acquire WMD.

A few states are dedicated proliferators, whose leaders are determined to develop, maintain, and improve their WMD and delivery capabilities, which directly threaten the United States, U.S. forces overseas, and/or our friends and allies. Because each of these regimes is different, we will pursue country-specific strategies that best enable us and our friends and allies to prevent, deter, and defend against WMD and missile threats from each of them. These strategies must also take into account the growing cooperation among proliferant states—so-called secondary proliferation—which challenges us to think in new ways about specific country strategies.

One of the most difficult challenges we face is to prevent, deter, and defend against the acquisition and use of WMD by terrorist groups. The current and potential future linkages between terrorist groups and state sponsors of terrorism are particularly dangerous and require priority attention. The full range of counter-proliferation, nonproliferation, and consequence management measures must be brought to bear against the WMD terrorist threat, just as they are against states of greatest proliferation concern.

END NOTE

Our National Strategy to Combat WMD requires much of all of us—the Executive Branch, the Congress, state and local governments, the American people, and our friends and allies. The requirements to prevent, deter, defend against, and respond to today's WMD threats are complex and challenging. But they are not daunting. We can and will succeed in the tasks laid out in this strategy; we have no other choice.